CLAIRE GROVE

Claire Grove is a Sony Radio Academy Award-winning radio producer who has created over three hundred dramas for BBC Radio 4, Radio 3 and the World Service. She produced *Classic Chandler*, a landmark series dramatising all eight Philip Marlowe novels, and *The Complete Ripley*. Awards include: Sony Gold for *A Woman in Waiting* by Thembi Mtshali, the story of a South African domestic worker; Sony Gold for *A Matter of Sex* by Nick Stafford; and a Silver Sony for *Banana Republic* by Greig Coetzee, one of three plays to mark ten years since the first democratic election in South Africa. Career highlights include working with Mike Bartlett on *Love Contract* and *Not Talking*, and with Charlotte Jones on *The Diva in Me*; directing Gary Oldman in *Walk Right By Me* by Christopher Harris, and Sir Patrick Stewart in Stephen Wyatt's *Double Jeopardy*; and recording Nick Darke's drama-documentary *Underground* in a Cornish tin mine.

STEPHEN WYATT

Stephen Wyatt is the only writer to have won the Tinniswood Award for best radio drama script twice – for *Memorials to the Missing* in 2007 and *Gerontius* in 2011. He's written over twenty original scripts for radio and numerous dramatisations. He's also written for television (*Doctor Who* and *Casualty*) and his theatre work has been seen everywhere from London's West End to the Bubble Theatre's touring tent. In conjunction with New Writing South and the University of Sussex, he created the UK's first online radio drama course in 2009. His first novel, *Big Dipper*, was published in 2012.

*

Claire and Stephen have worked together in radio for over ten years, beginning in 2001 with *Tales the Countess Told*. The original dramas they've collaborated on since include *Party Animal*, *Agnes Beaumont By Herself*, *Double Jeopardy* and *Strangers on a Film*, while their radio dramatisations include *Tom Jones*, *Vanity Fair*, *The Old Wives' Tale*, *Black Narcissus*, *The Complete Ripley* and *Classic Chandler*.

SO YOU WANT TO
WRITE RADIO DRAMA?

Claire Grove and Stephen Wyatt

NICK HERN BOOKS
London
www.nickhernbooks.co.uk

A Nick Hern Book

SO YOU WANT TO WRITE RADIO DRAMA?
first published in Great Britain in 2013
by Nick Hern Books Limited
The Glasshouse, 49a Goldhawk Road, London W12 8QP

Cover designed by Peter Bennett

Typeset by Nick Hern Books, London
Printed and bound in Great Britain by
CPI Group UK Ltd

A CIP catalogue record for this book
is available from the British Library

ISBN 978 1 84842 283 4

Contents

Appendices

Acknowledgements

Firstly, thanks to all the writers who have generously given permission for extracts from their work to be included in this book: Mike Bartlett for *Love Contract* (published as *Contractions*) and *Not Talking* (© Mike Bartlett and Methuen Drama, an imprint of Bloomsbury Publishing Plc.); Sebastian Baczkiewicz for *Pilgrim* (Series 2, Episode 3); The Dahl Estate and Charlotte Jones for *Matilda*; Carl Grose for *49 Donkeys Hanged* and *The Kneebone Cadillac*; Katie Hims for *Lost Property: The Wrong Label*; Charlotte Jones for *The Diva in Me*; Duncan Macmillan for *I Wish to Apologise for My Part in the Apocalypse*; Hattie Naylor for *Ivan and the Dogs* (© Hattie Naylor, 2010, reproduced by permission of United Agents, www.unitedagents.co.uk); Nick Perry for *The Loop* and Nick Warburton for *Prodigal Son* part of the Radio 4 *Witness* Series.

We would also like to thank Jeremy Howe, Commissioning Editor for Radio 4 Drama for allowing us to quote from the Radio 4 Commissioning Guidelines, Alex Boardman for permission to quote from his blog for BBC Writersroom and Steven Canny, BBC Executive Producer in Radio Comedy, for advice.

For reading and commenting on earlier drafts of this book, we are grateful to Sue Aldred, Christie Dickason and in particular Jeremy Mortimer.

Thanks to our editor at Nick Hern Books, Robin Booth, and to Matt Applewhite and Nick Hern himself for all their sound advice, support and enthusiasm.

Finally, this book is dedicated with love to our partners, Pete and Mark, who got us through it all.

Claire and Stephen

Introduction

This book is written by two people who have had a long-running love affair with radio drama. We have also enjoyed working together on a wide range of projects, both original plays and dramatisations, in a collaboration that goes back more than ten years.

But our experiences are different. Claire has been a senior radio drama producer for the BBC and has intimate and extensive working knowledge of the way in which radio plays are chosen, commissioned, edited and produced. She's also been responsible for encouraging writers new to radio and helping them to secure commissions.

Claire: I love radio drama. I am a shamelessly enthusiastic listener and I've had the enormous pleasure of working in it for many years as a producer and director. Why do I love it? Because it can take me anywhere the writer wants to take me. It gives me the freedom to imagine complete worlds. It can take me to places where I could never actually go in life. I love the vast range of subjects that it embraces and the sheer volume of it splurging out of the radio on a daily basis. Thrillers, romances, fantasy, gritty urban; there's something for everyone here. I love the fact that the word is king, that I can imagine complete characters from the timbre of an actor's voice and that a sudden silence can stop me in my tracks because I simply have to discover what happens next. And it fits in with a busy life. I can listen to it on my iPod while I'm walking, in the car while I'm driving, or at home while I'm doing other things.

Stephen is a freelance playwright who has been working in radio since the late 1970s, creating forty-five-, sixty- and ninety-minute original plays, as well as a wide range of dramatisations for radio. He's also taught a number of courses on radio drama and created the UK's first online radio drama course in collaboration with New Writing South and the University of Sussex.

Stephen: Where else would I have been allowed to write a play involving a talking Elgin Marble? Or allowed to burrow inside the minds of Alfred Hitchcock and Raymond Chandler? Or create a drama which moved between the nineteenth century, the present day and a Heaven filled with the music of Edward Elgar? There's something immensely liberating about the world of radio drama, and the people who work with you in it are a hundred per cent committed to doing the best for your play.

*

This is above all a practical book, written for anybody who feels they'd like to write a radio play, whether they're a first-time writer or a writer currently working in a different medium. It's also intended to be of help to anybody already involved in writing a radio play who wants some guidance on how to improve it or where to submit it.

It would be perfectly okay to read the book from cover to cover without doing any writing yourself – and hopefully you would still find out quite a lot about the process of how radio plays are written and made. But throughout we've also included a number of practical exercises, to encourage you to create your own radio drama. It's up to you, of course, how many of these exercises you do, what order you do them in or, indeed, whether you do them at all. But we both believe that if you're serious about wanting to write a radio drama, then the exercises will help you to explore and develop your ideas and get the most out of reading this book.

*

When we were planning this book, we both felt that it should reflect our shared knowledge of how radio drama works but also our very different perspectives on how radio plays get to be written and produced. We've therefore written in our own distinct voices about what each of us knows best.

But in the first part, we join together to explore just what makes radio drama such an exciting and inspiring medium to work in.

Claire and Stephen

PART ONE

What is Radio Drama?

CLAIRE AND STEPHEN

1

In the Beginning

In 1926, Gordon Lea's book *Radio Drama, and how to write it* was published in the George Allen & Unwin Practical Handbooks series. It carries a dedication 'To the BBC to whose enterprise is due the birth of a new art.' Lea's book was extraordinarily early in the field since what is generally agreed to have been radio's first specially written drama – *Danger*, by Richard Hughes, about a group of people trapped in a Welsh coal mine – had been broadcast in 1924, only two years previously.

Lea's comparisons are exclusively with the stage play. Films, after all, were still silent, while James Logie Baird was conducting the early experiments which would lead to the creation of television. Much of what Lea has to say is therefore badly dated, but it's impossible not to be struck by his enthusiasm for the imaginative possibilities of radio:

> Instead of a theatre capable of holding large numbers of people, we have an ordinary domestic room. For audience, actually hundreds of thousands of people, not gathered together in one place, but individualised in their own homes. Ultimately the audience is a vast number of individuals, geographically and psychologically disparate. By means of headphones or loud-speakers they 'listen' to the play. Objectively, they see nothing, but subjectively they can see everything. This is what the radio dramatist has to bear in mind.

He grasped the essential nature of the communication between writer and listener in the new medium:

> In conversation with a friend you can use a direct method, an intimate method, which would not be suitable for an orator's platform. The radio-play gains just this intimacy which a stage-play can never hope to have.

And he also understood the basic limitations:

> The medium of radio drama can offer positively the sound of the human voice and the sounds of nature, either actual or mechanically produced in imitation of nature. In other words, the means of interpreting the dramatist's work are the Human Voice, Music and Sound Effects.

Radio drama was just about to enter its first golden period. You can get some idea of it from the 1934 film *Death at Broadcasting House*, directed by Reginald Denham with a script based on a murder mystery co-written by the then head of radio drama, Val Gielgud, in which an unpopular actor is strangled on air during a broadcast (he's supposed to be alone in a studio at the time). Most of it was shot in a film studio rather than inside Broadcasting House, but it gives a strong flavour of how plays were recorded and the sense of occasion they created. Perhaps the most startling feature of the film is the night of the actual recording, when chauffeur-driven limousines deliver smart couples wearing full evening dress to the BBC Radio Theatre for all the world as if they were attending a West End first night.

Those glory days are gone but the announcements of the death of radio drama have proved again and again to be wildly exaggerated. It's survived the coming of sound to film, the advent of television (both black-and-white and colour), the inventions of the CD and the DVD and the rise of the internet. And, in all likelihood, it will survive whatever comes over the horizon next.

Perhaps that's partly because of the power of two distinctive features of radio drama which Gordon Lea identified in those early, heady days. One is its relationship with its audience. 'The radio drama does not make its appeal to a crowd but to an individual,' he wrote, although now in the computer era radio is far from alone in offering an experience direct to one person.

The other, however, is the enduring appeal of the medium for a playwright:

> Anything that is conceivable in his imagination is capable of complete expression and interpretation… If he wishes to set his play in the heart of a buttercup, the imagination of his hearer will provide the setting.

> This opens a new world to the dreamer of dreams.

2

Listening In

Do you listen to radio dramas? This may seem a strange question to start with but it is surprising how often people decide to have a go at fame and fortune in a field about which they know very little. There are people out there who imagine they are going to write a best-selling novel, a Hollywood screenplay or a long-running television series without seriously considering what's involved or the competitive nature of the field.

Anybody who believes they are going to get very rich or very famous by writing a radio play is obviously suffering from serious delusions of grandeur. Current fees for a first-time writer for a forty-five-minute Afternoon Drama, for example, stand at around £2,500. Thankfully, in our experience, most radio writers and most aspiring radio writers seem to have a grip on reality – and enjoy listening to radio dramas.

If you don't, you probably shouldn't have bought this book.

The enjoyment is very important but if you want to write a radio drama, you'll now be moving into a different and more analytical way of thinking about how it all works. Listening is an essential part of the learning process and, in tandem with your use of this book, we'd like you to keep on listening. Although there are occasional opportunities elsewhere to hear short experimental pieces or independent local drama broadcasts, for all intents and purposes this means listening to the radio drama output of the BBC, and it's on this that we concentrate throughout this book.

We also have a suggestion, which we hope will prove helpful. Keep a radio-drama diary. We don't want to dictate how you do this or set you homework you don't want to do, but we do believe that buying a notebook – or creating an online file – and recording your thoughts on what you've heard is something you should seriously consider. You'll find that, later on in the book, we'll both be making references to the ways in which such a record can be useful.

Keeping a Radio-drama Diary

Here's a possible framework for your radio-drama diary. For each drama you listen to, write down:

1. Title of play.

2. The drama slot (e.g. BBC Radio 4 Afternoon Drama) and the date of transmission.

3. The writer (of course).

4. The director/producer. (If you like their work, you might want to contact them one day.)

5. A brief outline of the story. (Try to keep it short and describe the content in such a way that it will enable you to remember the core of what happened later on. There's no doubt this is often difficult to achieve because it involves stepping back from the detail and trying to describe an overall concept. However, practising the skill involved will also help you with your own work. We promise.)

6. Notes on anything unusual or interesting in the treatment, e.g. the narrator was a tree, or the play shifted between the present and Ancient Egypt, or the effectiveness of a particular scene in its use of sound.

7. What you liked and didn't like about the play. (If
    possible, explore both, rather than just giving a
    thumbs up or thumbs down.)

Of course, you're not always going to have the time or the
inclination to do all these things, but do as much as you can
and as often as you can. There are a number of practical
exercises throughout this book, but in many ways keeping a
radio-drama diary is one of the most valuable things you
can do. You can learn about content, about technique and
about what is at the core of any given radio play. You will
also receive a constant reminder – and hopefully encour-
agement – about the huge variety of the plays being put out
and the often very different ways in which they handle the
conventions of radio.

So how do you find your way around the BBC Radio Drama
that's on offer?

The Drama Slots

BBC Radio 4 has the largest number of drama slots, sand-
wiched between news, features and documentaries, and
BBC Radio 3 has a flagship drama on Sunday nights. You
can listen live or via BBC iPlayer, where all radio dramas can
be found for up to seven days after broadcast. You can look
in the *Radio Times* or on the BBC website for detailed information about what's on, and every week there is a new
Drama of the Week Podcast and a Comedy Podcast available for download. You can sign up for these free podcasts
on the BBC website. But be warned, once you find it, this
stuff is very addictive.

The Afternoon Drama

There is nothing quite like the Afternoon Drama. Every weekday, Radio 4 broadcasts a forty-five-minute play following *The Archers*, the BBC's longest running soap. Nearly two hundred programmes are commissioned in this slot every year, two thirds of which are single dramas, and about forty of which are by first- or second-time writers to radio. This is where new writers usually start. The plays can be contemporary, period, comedy, thrillers, drama-documentary, poetry or anything else that you can think of. Writers can do virtually anything in the Afternoon Drama slot as long as they are telling the listener a good story, so here is a five-day sample taken at random from October 2012 to give you an idea of the range that is on offer:

- Monday: *Not Bobby* by award-winning writer Nick Warburton. A quirky satire about the education system in which a group of people try to educate a rabbit.

- Tuesday: *Collateral Damage*, the second play in a detective series created by Danny Brocklehurst and written by television writer Martin Jameson, in which DCI Stone investigates the death of a war veteran.

- Wednesday: *Power in Crimpsea* by Vicky Meer, a comedy drama in which the mayor of a fictional seaside town in the north-west of England hits on an ingenious way of reducing fuel costs whilst also boosting tourism.

- Thursday: *Top Kill* by award-winning writer Mike Walker. A hard-edged drama about the environmental devastation caused by cutting corners on an oil rig.

- Friday: *Rock and Doris and Elizabeth* by former *EastEnders* actress Tracy-Ann Oberman, exploring the relationship between Rock Hudson, Doris Day and Elizabeth Taylor, based on events in 1985 when Elizabeth Taylor launched an AIDS campaign and Rock Hudson's ravaged appearance shocked the world.

If you are new to writing radio drama this is the slot you should be aiming at.

Fifteen-minute dramas

This gets the largest audience of any drama slot on Radio 4 apart from *The Archers*. It is broadcast at 10.45 a.m. on weekdays, repeated at 7.45 p.m. It is a mixture of dramatisations and new writing, usually commissioned in batches of five. It has to grab the listeners and deliver story and characters simply and powerfully in a very short amount of time. Audiences don't usually hear every episode so each one has to be satisfying in itself, as well as creating an air of suspense to encourage them to return the next day. No mean feat in under fifteen minutes. It is sometimes known as the *Woman's Hour* drama because it is first broadcast as part of that programme, but that doesn't mean that the material has to be solely aimed at women. There are a lot of male listeners too. Also, the drama has to work for the evening audience which has just been listening to the arts programme *Front Row*. Here is a sample of what you'll find in this slot:

- *Tales of the City*, an account of the sexual mores of 1980s San Francisco, by Armistead Maupin, dramatised by Bryony Lavery.

- *HighLites*, a comedy crime series set in a hairdressers', by Steve Chambers and Phil Nodding.

- *Not a Love Story* by Shelagh Stephenson, in which a woman decides whether or not to report a rape. We follow her decision and the devastating consequences.

- A dramatisation by Pat Cumper of Alice Walker's *The Color Purple*, which won a Sony Radio Academy Award (the radio equivalent of the Oscars).

- *Q & A*, based on the novel by Vikas Swarup, which inspired the film *Slumdog Millionaire*, brilliantly adapted by dramatist Ayeesha Menon and director John Dryden. The story revolves around an Indian boy from the slums who goes on a game show. In each episode the boy faces a new question, creating a sense of escalating tension and mounting stakes: will he or won't he be able to come up with the answer? And he is a kind and honourable character in a corrupt world so we are automatically rooting for him. The game-show storyline is intercut with incidents from the boy's past which reveal how he knows each answer. It was a completely gripping piece of storytelling, and it went on to win a Sony Award.

A first-time writer is unlikely to be commissioned in this slot, although it's not impossible if the idea is outstanding and you have plenty of evidence of top-quality writing to back it up.

Comedy narrative: morning, evening and night

The 11.30 a.m. slot on Radio 4 is usually a narrative comedy drama, panel game or occasionally a dramatisation of something well-loved and familiar, such as an Agatha Christie detective novel. It is a mid-morning comforter for an audience that is busy doing other things. It is thirty minutes in length and usually in series of between three and six episodes. Good examples include:

- *Cabin Pressure*, a comedy series by John Finnemore, featuring the ups and downs of a small airline. The crew are forever getting lost, landing in the wrong place and generally cocking up.

- *HR* by Nigel Williams, in which two paranoid older men who work for a large organisation are in mortal fear that their laziness and ineptitude will be exposed by the secretary outside their door.

- *Miles Jupp: In and Out of the Kitchen*, in which writer Miles Jupp also plays the central character, a minor celebrity chef. In a media-driven world he is struggling to hang on to his dignity, his relationship with his partner Anthony and his ability to come up with great recipes.

Radio 4 commissioning editors want comedies that will come back time and time again in this slot, but each episode has to be self-contained. Experienced comedy writers are most likely to get commissioned here.

There is another thirty-minute comedy slot at 6.30 p.m. on weekdays. Some of the programmes here are panel games and sketch shows but you will also find narrative comedy such as the spoof historical drama *Bleak Expectations* by Mark Evans, and the hugely popular *Old Harry's Game* written by, and starring, Andy Hamilton as the Devil who interferes in the lives of mortals in every possible way. This slot is about simple, clear storylines and little else at a time of day when the audience is at its busiest. Big-name comedy writers get commissioned here.

There is a relatively new thirty-minute comedy slot at 7.15 p.m. on Sundays. This is mostly themed series featuring well-known performers such as Marcus Brigstocke or David Sedaris. Occasionally it features a sitcom such as *The Golden Age*, set in 1930s Broadcasting House, by television writer Arthur Matthews (*Father Ted, Brass Eye*).

The late-night slot at 11 p.m. is where less experienced writers can find their radio legs and where established writers are encouraged to try something new. This is not just a comedy slot. It is a performance space for idiosyncratic voices at a time of day when listeners are prepared to try something a bit different. Programmes can be fifteen or thirty minutes long and can be commissioned as single dramas or series. Good examples include:

- *I Regress*, written by and starring Matt Berry, who plays a sadistic regression therapist. Each episode sees him dealing with a different client. It was dark, funny and original.

- *Terry Pratchett's Eric*, a spoof version of the Faust story dramatised by Robin Brooks from the Discworld novel.

- *Warhorses of Letters* by Robert Hudson and Marie Phillips. Starring Stephen Fry, this was the love story of two gay horses who write to each other. It was gloriously silly and couldn't have worked anywhere else but on radio.

If you are new to writing comedy and you have a great idea, this is the slot where you are most likely to be commissioned.

Saturday Drama

This is the matinee slot on Radio 4. It is about enjoyment and escapism. It's the film or theatre show that you wanted to buy a ticket for. It is usually sixty minutes long and starts at 2.30 p.m. This is where Raymond Chandler's *Philip Marlowe* novels were aired and John le Carré's *Smiley* novels were dramatised. This is where you'll find James Bond, or a radical new version of Lewis Carroll's *Through the Looking Glass* dramatised by Stephen Wyatt, or a complete season of ten Swedish novels by Per Wahlöö and Maj Sjöwall featuring Martin Beck, the curmudgeonly detective who is a forerunner to Ian Rankin's Inspector Rebus and Henning Mankell's Wallander. This is also the slot for intelligent storytelling by the best writers in Britain. New dramas by Peter Flannery, Charlotte Jones or David Hare

are aired here alongside adaptations of classic theatre plays such as Howard Brenton's *Bloody Poetry* or Henrik Ibsen's *Hedda Gabler*.

Classic Serial

This slot more or less does what it says on the tin: dramatisations of substantial, well-known novels in two or three parts. Starting at 3 p.m. on Sunday afternoons, each episode is repeated the following Saturday at 9 p.m. Typical dramatisations include Alexandre Dumas' *The Count of Monte Cristo* adapted by Sebastian Baczkiewicz, *The Heat of the Day* by Elizabeth Bowen adapted by Harold Pinter, and *The History of Titus Groan*, based on Mervyn Peake's fantasy novels, a big, bold, brilliant series in six episodes by Brian Sibley. The Classic Serial slot also occasionally offers radical takes on much-loved books, for example Sony Award-winning writer Ayeesha Menon's reworking of Charles Dickens' *Martin Chuzzlewit* set amongst the Catholic community in modern-day Mumbai, India. The slot may also include lesser-known classics from world literature such as *Pather Panchali: Song of the Road* by Bibhutibhushan Bandyopadhyay, dramatised by Tanika Gupta. First published in 1929, this Bengali novel depicts a poor family's struggle to survive in their ancestral rural home seen from the point of view of Apu, their bookish young son. A 1955 film version by Satyajit Ray is today considered one of the greatest films ever made.

Very occasionally the Classic Serial slot offers dramatisations of non-fiction. Claire produced an extraordinarily popular two-part version of Boswell's *Life of Johnson* dramatised by Robin Brooks. Its popularity may have been partly due to the fact that many Radio 4 listeners have the book on their shelves and feel they ought to know what's in it. Another non-fiction example is *Songs and Lamentations from the Old Testament*, in which poet Michael Symmons Roberts interwove the sensual love poetry of the *Song of Songs* with the violence and vengeance of the *Book of Lamentations*. It is rare that an inexperienced writer gets considered in this slot, but it is possible if you can show that you are uniquely qualified to dramatise the particular book you have chosen.

The Archers

Set in the fictional English village of Ambridge, *The Archers* is the world's longest running radio soap. With over five million listeners, it is the most listened-to Radio 4 programme apart from the news, and it holds the radio record for online listening too. It inspires huge loyalty from its devoted followers. There is an *Archers* fan club, an *Archers* roadshow, a podcast and even a spin-off series called *Ambridge Extra* on the BBC's digital station Radio 4 Extra.

The Archers is broadcast on Radio 4 on Sundays to Fridays at 7 p.m., repeated the next day at 2 p.m., except on Saturdays. If you want to catch a whole week's worth in one go there's an omnibus edition on Sundays at 10 a.m. Each episode is thirteen minutes long. *Ambridge Extra* is broadcast on Radio 4 Extra on Tuesdays and Thursdays at 2.15 p.m., with an omnibus half-hour programme on Sundays at 11.15 a.m. and again at 7.15 p.m.

As with all soaps, the hook for the audience is the characters. They behave in mostly predictable ways, but they must go in different directions every now and then or the audience will get bored. At the heart of the programme are solid and reliable David and Ruth Archer at Brookfield Farm. They deal with current farming issues such as organic food production and badger culling. The prosperous Aldridges are money-driven practitioners of the agribusiness. Brian, the head of the family, is a serial adulterer. The Grundys, formerly struggling tenant farmers who were brought to prominence in the late 1970s and early 1980s as comic characters, are now seen as a rural underclass doggedly battling adversity. Pretentious and domineering 'townie' Lynda Snell is the butt of many jokes, although her sheer energy, particularly organising the fête and the panto, make her a stalwart of the series. Then there are the nice-but-dim village squires, the Pargetters, who own Lower Loxley Hall. Nigel Pargetter's death falling from a roof sent shockwaves through *Archers* fans, but his wife Elizabeth carries on his commitment to environmentalism. At the younger end there is Tom Archer, and we follow his chequered love life and the ups and downs of his sausage business.

The Archers is written by a small number of writers. Occasionally they take on a new writer but soap teams tend to stick together for years. Teamwork is very important. The writers not only have to know the characters but also write to agreed storylines, picking up threads where the writers of the previous episodes have left off.

Drama on 3

BBC Radio 3 has a Sunday evening drama slot, usually ninety minutes, which broadcasts a mixture of classical adaptations of, for instance, Shakespeare, Chekhov or Ibsen, and new plays by established contemporary writers such as David Edgar, Caryl Churchill or Simon Stephens. This is the slot where regional audiences get access to successful plays from the Royal Court or the National Theatre, usually with their original director and cast. There is also new writing to be found here but it is unlikely that the writer wouldn't have written anything before. The Radio 3 audience is not large but they are sharp, well-informed critics. They are used to listening to lengthy classical music programmes and they have often chosen to make a special date with the drama rather than just come across it while doing something else. A random sample of Radio 3 dramas broadcast in October 2012 includes: *The Strange Case of the Man in the Velvet*

Jacket, Robert Forrest's play based on Robert Louis Steven-
son's early life in Edinburgh, *Mary Stuart* by Friedrich
Schiller in a new version by David Harrower, and *The Torch-
bearers*, in which award-winning poet and dramatist Simon
Armitage captured our extraordinary relationship with the
Olympic flame. This was broadcast live – a rarity in Radio
Drama – from the Free Thinking Festival at the Baltic Cen-
tre in Newcastle.

The Wire

This is an occasional series of radical dramas on Saturdays
on Radio 3: contemporary, stylish and provocative. Pushing
the boundaries of form and content, it is the Royal Court
Upstairs or the Paines Plough of the airwaves. Writers are
encouraged to take a risk here. A Wire play can be a monologue, a comedy or a dramatic poem. It is usually sixty
minutes in length. If the Afternoon Drama is too full of
middle-class angst for your taste, then try listening to this.
Examples include:

- *Iced* by poet Kate Clancy, in which a teen eco-blogger
from Finland wins a competition to join a low-carbon
expedition to the North Pole. Blogging her way across
the Arctic, she has to navigate deadly cracks in the ice
as well as environmental controversy.

- *Everything Between Us* by award-winning Irish
playwright David Ireland, a bold and original comic
drama about two estranged sisters who come to blows
on the first day of a new Truth and Reconciliation
Commission in Northern Ireland.

- Jack Thorne's *People Snogging in Public Places*, about a
family looking after an uncle with learning
difficulties, seen from the viewpoint of his nephew.
Raw, funny and touching, with robust language, it
won a Sony Award for best drama in 2010.

Radio 4 Extra

This digital station broadcasts repeats of comedies and dramas. They do commission a tiny number of new programmes but if you are an inexperienced writer you won't get considered here. What Radio 4 Extra is brilliant for is catching up with programmes that you have missed. You can find anything from *The Navy Lark* through to the latest cutting-edge drama, and you can completely immerse yourself in a warm bath of plays, comedy and readings, uninterrupted by news and documentaries. A typical sample might include the narrative comedy *A Charles Paris Mystery* by Simon Brett starring Bill Nighy as an actor-cum-sleuth, *I, Claudius* by Robert Graves repeated from Radio 4's Classic Serial, *Incredible Women* by Jeremy Front, a spoof fifteen-minute documentary series starring Rebecca Front, and archive repeats of *Steptoe and Son* by Ray Galton and Alan Simpson from 1966.

Building a Database

When you hear a production that you like, listen to the end credits and make a note of the name of the producer and where they are based. You can also find this information in the *Radio Times* and on BBC iPlayer. Put this in your radio-drama diary so you begin to build a database of people you want to contact in the future with your script.

BBC in-house drama is made by BBC producers in London, Birmingham, Manchester, Cardiff, Bristol, Edinburgh and Belfast. There is a list of their addresses in the Resources section at the end of this book. Producers in all these centres are interested in finding new writers, so as well as noting the ones whose work you like, it makes sense to familiarise yourself with what is being made in the drama office that is nearest to you. All the information you need is on air, online and in the *Radio Times*.

At the end of a drama, the producer's name may be followed by that of an independent company, e.g. Pacificus, Goldhawk or Sweet Talk. About forty per cent of BBC radio drama is made by independent companies. Many of them are small and only make their own work, but some of them are interested in finding new writers. There is a list of them in the Resources section of this book and their websites will point you towards who to contact.

When the time comes to submit your script and ideas, you use more or less the same approach with any producer, whether they are BBC or an independent. We deal with submitting your work in Part Three of this book, but at this stage gathering names of who to contact and finding out what you do and don't like is a key part of preparing for your future as a writer.

BBC Writersroom

If you do only one thing to get a better insight into writing for radio, television, film, and the theatre then visit the BBC Writersroom website, www.bbc.co.uk/writersroom. Created and led by Kate Rowland, an ex-head of BBC Radio Drama and commissioning editor for Radio 3's The Wire, it is the BBC's official entry point for new writers. The role of Writersroom is to find and develop relationships with talented writers and link them to producers within the industry.

The BBC Writersroom website is packed with useful information about writing for film, television and theatre, and there is a special section on radio drama. They offer step-by-step writing tips and you can send them a script and get feedback on it (see the website for details of submission rounds). There is a wide range of radio-drama scripts available to download and they have lots of information about competitions, events and writing opportunities both inside and outside the BBC. They also run a very entertaining blog with behind-the-scenes insights from television and radio writers, and you can sign up for their newsletter. But most importantly the website is updated all the time so it is the most reliable source of information about what is currently on offer for writers.

It also has regularly updated interviews with experienced writers talking about a huge range of subjects, from writer's block to creating a feature film. Typical examples are Lucy Gannon talking about how she got started (she went in for a competition), Roy Williams and Jimmy McGovern tackling writer's block, Tony Marchant on creating a series and Jack Thorne on the drama that changed his life (it was *Boys from the Blackstuff* by Alan Bleasdale).

3

What is Radio Drama?

In this chapter, we're going to start thinking about the nature of radio drama, its strengths and its drawbacks as a dramatic form.

What does radio do well?

Take some time to think about your experience of listening to radio drama. In what ways is it different from watching a film, a television programme or a play in the theatre? What does radio do well? Are there perhaps things it does very well? And some things it doesn't do well at all?

If you can, make a few notes of your ideas before moving on to the next section, where we outline our own thoughts on what does and doesn't work well in radio drama. There may be things on your list which we don't discuss or even mention. We're not aiming to create a definitive list, only beginning to explore the creative possibilities of the medium you want to write for.

Radio drama takes place inside your head, not in front of your eyes. It's what gives it its wonderful freedom, both for the writer and for the listener, but it's also why some things you might like to do simply won't work in radio.

The bad news first

Let's begin by looking at some of the things radio drama doesn't do well:

1. Any sort of big lavish spectacle, battle, riot or teeming social event which depends for its effect upon us being able to see and appreciate the scale of what's happening. Of course, radio can suggest armies on the march, pitched battles, cheering crowds thronging the streets and the ball to end all balls with a few evocative sound effects, but there's not going to be a gasp of surprise or joy from the audience.

   This became clear to us when we were working together on a radio dramatisation of Thackeray's novel, *Vanity Fair*. In any stage, screen or television version of the book, one of the big set pieces is the Duchess of Richmond's ball on the eve of the Battle of Waterloo. It's a chance to display aristocratic ladies in beautiful frocks and officers in magnificent military uniforms, descending staircases and dancing beneath chandeliers in a glittering ballroom. We were pretty convinced that this was going to be a key scene in the radio version. But when it came to it, we had a bit of a shock. We realised that there could be music and there could be crowd noises and listeners would know we were at a ball, but there was no way to make it any more impressive than that. Our big scene wasn't a big scene any more.

   The result was that the scenes at the ball focused almost exclusively on the main characters and particularly on Becky Sharp's attempts to entrap the fickle George Osborne (destined to die on the field of Waterloo) into eloping with her and abandoning their respective spouses. Which, in storytelling terms, was no bad thing. However, there was little glamour or breathtaking visual magic about what was going on.

2. Linked to this, Hollywood-style car chases are also out. Cinema audiences may gasp as cars nearly collide or race over bridges just before the bridges collapse

into the river below. But in radio, this comes down to some car noises and a commentary which would have to spell out what doesn't need to be spelled out in visual terms ('Oh no, I can't believe it... The bridge looks like it's collapsing... Not sure I'm going to make it!', etc.).

More seriously, anything which needs a very detailed physical choreography isn't going to work on radio. The silent sequence in which the hooded stalker pursues the heroine relentlessly through the forest is never going to make an impact on radio. There are other ways of doing it on radio, but not that way.

Related to this is the idea, which may at first seem odd, that scenes involving sex and/or violence are often more disturbing on radio than on film or television. Given only sounds to trigger the imagination, some listeners can draw on their own experience and create mental pictures far more shocking and graphic than was intended or even suggested. Radio doesn't have the same control as film or television over what is being conveyed in physical terms. Which, again, is both good and bad.

A favourite story on this topic comes from a producer who received a letter about a radio drama she'd worked on from a listener who said she had been so disgusted by what she'd heard that she had had to switch the radio off. The letter ended, slightly plaintively, asking if the producer could tell her what happened next.

3. By and large, radio doesn't work well if there are more than three people in any given scene. This is basically a matter of how many voices a listener can follow and still keep track of who they are and what they're saying. Skilful casting, of course, can make characters more distinctive so that listeners will then find it

easier to tell the voices apart. But a basic problem remains: without visual information, it's very difficult to understand a conversation or argument taking place between, say, five or six people.

In a film or theatre, a 'silent presence', somebody who is present and says nothing, can be very powerful. The fact that they say nothing can add a real tension to the scene. We are waiting for their intervention, or realise the arguments they're hearing are totally irrelevant to them.

In radio, there is no magic in a silent presence. Unless the person present is kept in our minds (e.g. 'But you've said nothing for the last five minutes'), then as far as the listeners are concerned, they don't exist. In any case, too many voices clamouring for attention can only lead to confusion.

Radio is not therefore – to take a silly example – the ideal place for a wedding reception scene in which dozens of people related to the bride and groom erupt into very specific recriminations and punch-ups.

There's more, inevitably, but let's move on to –

The good news

To repeat, radio drama takes place inside your head, not in front of your eyes. Which means:

1. As a writer you have a very intimate relationship with the listener. You talk softly into the listener's ear. There's no need to shout or lecture. The words you have written will be heard in the same way as the words of a poem. Of course, the actor's voice interprets – as it does with any oral performance of a poem, even by the author – and the producer and sound engineer choose the sound effects, but there

are no visuals to draw the listener away from the words and sounds which the writer has imagined. The communication is therefore much more direct and personal than it can ever be with theatre or television.

2.   From both the writer's and listener's point of view, this relationship is very precious. And it means that the writer's individual voice is valued in a way which is rare in television. Of course, radio has its very own soap opera and offers plays which are social-realist (no bad thing if they go where conventional television won't go), but at the centre of most of its original drama is an opportunity for a writer to speak with the voice that is theirs and no one else's. There's a place for this in theatre, of course, but in radio many many more people will be listening to what you have to say.

3.   You can set your play anywhere, any time, with a cast of thousands. We've already talked about the downside of this: spectacle doesn't work on radio. But the positive aspect is good news. You want five thousand Egyptians worshipping their Pharaoh before a completed Pyramid? You wish to create one of the battles of the English Civil War or the American War of Independence? You want a polite dinner party swept away by a tidal flood? Or a dog swallowing the whole of North Wales? None of these things present any great problem, particularly given the skills of most sound engineers and their teams.

'I like radio for the pictures' is the cliché. But the budgetary restraints upon your imagination really are very minimal. If you can imagine it in terms of words and sound effects then it can be achieved.

But previous cautions do apply. The five thousand Egyptians are just background noise. Where's your focus? On the Pharaoh and his architect? On one of the slave labourers and his best friend? You can juxtapose the two, of course, but you're never going to take anybody's breath away with your recreated Pyramid.

4.   Is there any other dramatic medium in which you could quite plausibly choose to make a doughnut your principal character? Or a chair? A picture painted by Rubens? The ghost of a dog?

And if we're talking human beings, how about a hundred-and-fifty-year-old woman? Or a long-dead Holy Roman Emperor who wants to get out of his tomb and sort out the modern world? Or a hermaphrodite who's signed up for a course with the Open University on gender politics?

The freedom can sometimes be frightening. Most of us choose to stay closer to home. But it's still true that in radio drama the world is your oyster. Or indeed an oyster's world could be your radio play.

And here's another consideration. When you go to the theatre or the cinema, you buy a ticket and it's a big decision to walk out; but nobody is forcing you to keep on listening to a radio play you're not interested in. Which leads us to…

4

Openings

People can listen to a radio drama anywhere. They can be doing the ironing. They can be driving along a motorway. They can be waiting for a kettle to boil or painting a room. They can be repairing a car or working on their computer. And, these days, they don't have to be listening at the same time as the play is transmitted: they can pick it up at any time in the next week via BBC iPlayer.

That's the power of radio drama. It's available at all times and in all places. And the audience isn't required to sit down and watch. But with that power comes a challenge. There is no such thing as a 'captive' audience, compelled to listen to what's going on in your radio drama come what may. The listeners haven't paid for a ticket; they have other things to bother about, and if they're bored or distracted by something else, they can switch off or simply switch radio channels.

So how do you get the listener's attention and how do you hold it?

This chapter is about ear-catching openings. On radio, it's very easy for a listener to lose interest or switch off if their attention isn't caught in the first few minutes. So, within those two or three minutes, a writer has not only to capture the listener's attention but also let them know something about the nature and tone of the piece.

We've chosen some openings for you to consider. The first is from playwright Duncan Macmillan's first play for radio, *I Wish to Apologise for My Part in the Apocalypse*. It was first broadcast in July 2008, produced by Sam Hoyle with Bill Nighy as Keith. It's a piece which begins almost literally with a bang and offers an opening speech which is both startling and intriguing.

(We'll return to this topic of radio-script conventions more fully in Part Four, but the term 'V.O'. or 'voice-over' describes when a character is talking directly to the listeners or expressing their inner thoughts instead of being involved in a scene with other characters. 'FX' stands for 'sound effects'.)

Opening One

From *I Wish to Apologise for My Part in the Apocalypse* by Duncan Macmillan

SCENE 1

FX:	A DEEP, OMINOUS RUMBLE. AN INTERPLANETARY COLLISION. THE END OF THE WORLD.
KEITH:	(V.O.) *I've learnt a lot since the world ended. Mostly, I've learnt to stop taking things for granted. I know there's nothing that can be done about it now, but I want to explain how the world came to an end and to take some responsibility. I wish to apologise for my part in the apocalypse.*
FX:	THE RUMBLE REACHES ITS CONCLUSION AND SUBSIDES.
KEITH:	(V.O.) *It all began on my wife's fiftieth birthday.*

SCENE 2

<u>FX:</u>	<u>A RADIO IS PLAYING NEARBY – VAN MORRISON'S 'MOONDANCE'. SOMEONE MOWS THEIR LAWN. CHILDREN ARE PLAYING. DISTANT TRAFFIC.</u>
TILDA:	What's this?
KEITH:	It's a present.
TILDA:	It's a big one.
KEITH:	Happy birthday.
TILDA:	Thank you.
KEITH:	Open it.
TILDA:	I don't know what to say.
KEITH:	Open it.
TILDA:	What on earth is it?
KEITH:	Would you just open it?
<u>FX:</u>	<u>SHE DOES</u>.
KEITH:	Well?
TILDA:	What on earth is it?
KEITH:	Happy birthday.
TILDA:	Yes, but
KEITH:	Happy fiftieth my darling.
TILDA:	Yes but, what is this?
KEITH:	It's a telescope.
TILDA:	Oh.
KEITH:	You hate it.

TILDA:	No, it's just
KEITH:	I knew you'd hate it.
TILDA:	It's not that, it's just
KEITH:	What?
TILDA:	Well, what in the world made you think I'd want this?
KEITH:	Well, I
TILDA:	It's my fiftieth birthday.
KEITH:	I know and I wanted to
TILDA:	It's fifty years since I was born.
KEITH:	I know and
TILDA:	A half-century.
KEITH:	Yes, I know
TILDA:	It's kind of a special occasion.
KEITH:	Of course, I know that I
TILDA:	How much did this cost?
KEITH:	Well
TILDA:	Please tell me it wasn't expensive.
KEITH:	Well
TILDA:	Please tell me you kept a receipt. Unbelievable.
KEITH:	(V.O.) *Things escalated. They always do. She went upstairs and –*
FX:	A DOOR SLAMS.

Within a couple of minutes, Macmillan's play has deftly moved from the apocalypse to a marital argument over a fiftieth-birthday present. The play is a romantic comedy about the end of the world. Tilda goes on to use her telescope and falls in love with the moon. Her husband is at first jealous then baffled. It seems the moon is getting closer. Planes cannot fly, tides cease so shipping is in trouble and the Earth is burning up. As the title suggests, Keith narrates all this from a time after the planet has gone into meltdown. We know none of this at the start but the hints are there, tantalising, funny and sinister.

*

Can you think of any radio plays you've listened to recently when you were hooked right from the start? Have a look in your (very useful) radio-drama diary.

We've provided two more openings for you to consider. As you read each of them, ask yourself some questions. Make notes if it helps:

1. Does this opening make you want to listen on?

2. Do you get an idea of what the play is going to be about?

3. What makes an opening effective?

The second opening is from *Lost Property: The Wrong Label* by Katie Hims, an Afternoon Drama first broadcast in May 2011 and produced by Jessica Dromgoole. It was the first of a trilogy by the writer which followed members of a family from World War Two to the present day, and it was broadcast over three consecutive days. The second play, *The Year My Mother Went Missing*, won a BBC Award for the Best Audio & Music Drama in 2012.

The play is set in London in 1941. Ray and Queenie are children. Alice is their mother. They have light London accents.

Opening Two

From *The Wrong Label* by Katie Hims

<u>SCENE 1</u>

<u>FX:</u>	<u>EXTERIOR. EXPLOSIONS. SHOUTING.</u>
	<u>CROSS-FADE TO INTERIOR. ANDERSON SHELTER.</u>
RAY:	Queenie.
QUEENIE:	Yeah?
RAY:	You know when you die.
QUEENIE:	Yeah.
RAY:	What do you think it feels like?
QUEENIE:	Depends how you die doesn't it.
RAY:	No but do you think you can feel it happening?
QUEENIE:	Well that depends how quick it is.
RAY:	I suppose.
QUEENIE:	If there's no time. If you just get like wiped out in a flash how can you feel anything at all?
RAY:	I don't know.
ALICE:	Ray. Queenie.
RAY:	Yeah?
QUEENIE:	Yeah?
ALICE:	Stop talking about death.
RAY:	We can't help it.
QUEENIE:	We can't stop ourselves.

ALICE:	Play a game. Play I Spy.
QUEENIE:	In here?
ALICE:	Why not?
QUEENIE:	There's nothing to spy except spiders.
RAY:	What do you think Hitler is doing right now?
ALICE:	I've no idea.
QUEENIE:	Probably having his tea. In peace. With no bombs or anything.
ALICE:	I hope my wedding china is alright.
QUEENIE:	But you never use it.
ALICE:	Because I don't want it to get smashed.
QUEENIE:	If you never use it you're not going to miss it are you?
ALICE:	I like looking at it. I just like looking at it.
FX:	A TODDLER STARTS TO CRY, JUST A LITTLE BIT.
ALICE:	Sssh Ella May. Don't be scared Ella May. See you've scared Ella May now.
QUEENIE:	How have we scared Ella May?
ALICE:	Talking about death.
QUEENIE:	She doesn't even know what death is.
FX:	ELLA MAY CRIES AGAIN. ALICE STARTS TO SING TO HER.
RAY:	(WHISPERING) Queenie?
QUEENIE:	Yeah?
RAY:	If we die.

QUEENIE:	Yeah.
RAY:	Tonight. I mean if we die tonight.
QUEENIE:	Yeah.
RAY:	Do you think we'll go straight to Heaven?
QUEENIE:	I don't know.
RAY:	I don't want to go to purgatory.
QUEENIE:	I don't want to go to purgatory either.
RAY:	Maybe if you get killed by a bomb you can just skip that bit and go straight to Heaven. As like a reward.
QUEENIE:	Maybe.
RAY:	If we knew then I wouldn't mind thinking about the dying bit.
QUEENIE:	Maybe we're dead already.
RAY:	Do you think we are?
QUEENIE:	Maybe we died and we just don't know it and this is purgatory.

Again the play starts with noise and explosions, but then introduces us immediately to an intimate scene inside the air-raid shelter with the hushed matter-of-fact voices of two small children discussing death.

Did you want to listen on? Did you get a feel for what the play is going to be about?

*

The third extract is from the third series of Sebastian Baczkiewicz's fantasy drama *Pilgrim*, broadcast in February 2012 in the Afternoon Drama slot, produced by Marc Beeby, who co-produces the series with Jessica Dromgoole. It won a Special Commendation at the Prix Europa Festival for the Best European Television, Radio and Online productions and was nominated for the Prix Italia Awards, the oldest and most prestigious international competition for Radio, television and web programmes.

Opening Three

From *Pilgrim* (Series 3, Episode 2) by Sebastian Baczkiewicz

<u>SCENE 1</u>	<u>**INTERIOR. BIRDIE BIRD'S HOUSE**</u>
<u>FX:</u>	<u>BARRY AND BIRDIE ARE IN HER KITCHEN. BARRY SITS AT A TABLE EATING SOME STEW. RAIN HAMMERS DOWN OUTSIDE. A FIRE CRACKLES IN THE GRATE.</u>
BARRY:	…my dad was a Tammy Wynette fan.
BIRDIE:	He was?
BARRY:	Massive. Married five times y'know.
BIRDIE:	Your dad?
BARRY:	Tammy.
BIRDIE:	More stew?
BARRY:	If it's going..
<u>FX:</u>	<u>BIRDIE POURS SOME MORE STEW. BARRY EATS.</u>
BARRY:	Amazing, Birdie. The meat. Delicious.
<u>FX:</u>	<u>BARRY BLOWS A KISS WITH HIS FINGERS.</u>

BIRDIE:	You're married aren't you, Barry?
FX:	BARRY SEASONS THE STEW.
BARRY:	Met my Mary back in the summer of eighty-five and never looked back. Childhood sweethearts us. Careless whisper.
BIRDIE:	No D.I.V.O.R.C.E in the happy house of Barry Leaming then?
BARRY:	Not quite sure what you're driving at there, Birdie.
BIRDIE:	You'd never play a person false. Deliberately sell them, I don't know, a car you knew to be faulty.
BARRY:	I thought I was here to talk about replacing your shed windows.
BIRDIE:	William Palmer.
BARRY:	Who?
BIRDIE:	Best have him back here as soon as you possibly can or it will all be a bit late for the spell to be put right.
BARRY:	For the what to be… what?
BIRDIE:	For the spell that's going to completely – and by completely I do mean completely – transform you into a hare in a year and a day from, well, today.
BARRY:	Into a hare?
FX:	THERE IS A SLIGHT PAUSE – THEN THEY LAUGH.
BARRY:	You had me going there, Birdie.

BIRDIE: Eat up.

BARRY: Not rabbit is it? And I did warn you about
             that car. Said its engine needed a look at. I
             did.

BIRDIE: You did, Barry. You did. Colonel Coburn's
             going to do all he can for you but it's him,
             and only him, who can help you. I need you
             to remember that.

BARRY: Help me how?

FX: SUDDENLY BARRY PUSHES HIS CHAIR
             BACK, SPLUTTERING.

BARRY: What have you… my head's spinning…
             what have you-tchick – done to me?

BIRDIE: You know I would love for you and I to talk
             Tammy all night, Barry, but unfortunately you
             don't have a minute to spare.

FX: BARRY RUNS HOWLING TO THE DOOR.

BIRDIE: Don't forget the name now – William Palmer.

LITTLE GIRL: Of
             All the tales told on
             These islands few are as
             Strange as that of William
             Palmer cursed, apparently
             On the road to Canterbury
             In the spring of 1180
             Five for denying the presence of the
             Other world by the King of the
             Greyfolk, or faerie, himself and
             Compelled to walk from that day
             To this between the worlds of magic

> And of men and subsequently known
> In all the strange and wonderful lore
> Attributed to the mysterious
> William Palmer
> As
> Pilgrim

These three openings are very different but each of them introduces us quickly and confidently into a world which we sense the writer understands.

In Sebastian Baczkiewicz's series, Pilgrim (played by Paul Hilton) is humanity's ageless champion against the supernatural. On one level, the opening scene between Birdie and Barry, with its chat about Tammy Wynette, stew and shed windows, seems quite normal. But the supernatural is already being hinted at in the references to Palmer and the spells to transform Barry into a hare. A small child then tells us more about William Palmer himself so that we know who Pilgrim is and what his mission consists of. This is an arresting and unusual device used throughout the series to set up the world that Pilgrim inhabits, where everyday reality and magic clash, and demon children and assorted other characters drop through time.

If you were coming to the *Pilgrim* series for the first time, would this opening make you listen on? Are you grabbed by the strange juxtapositions in the world of Birdie and Barry?

Over to You

Once you've had a chance to think about these openings, take the opportunity if you can to come up with
your own ear-catching opening. Don't ask yourself
where it's going. Just try to get the listener's attention.

Here's an exercise that might help. Don't take more
than five minutes over it. Don't hesitate. Write down
what comes into your head.

Think of a sound effect – a bell ringing, a burglar alarm,
a dog barking. Write it down.

Then think of a line of dialogue. Don't take too long.
Write it down.

Then think of another contrasting sound effect.

Think of another line of dialogue. It could be from the
same character or it could be from somebody else.

Now think of a final sound effect. It could be small (a
fly buzzing) or it could be large (a volcano erupts).

That's your first radio play. And your first opening.

If you enjoyed doing this exercise, do it as often as you
like.

You're thinking about how dialogue and sound work
together. And about how you get a radio audience's
attention.

Note from Claire

When I used this exercise in South Africa, one of the
writers chose the sound of trains passing. This grew
into a ten-minute play about a woman from the rural
areas whose husband works in the gold mines in
Johannesburg. Their relationship is framed by the train

journeys which take him away. They are young and in love, but as the years go by she ends up bringing up two children alone, going to meet him at the train station every six months, becoming less and less able to recognise the man she married. And one day he doesn't come. The station guard gives her a lift home in his Peugeot. He has loved her since they were at school together. He is kind. They become good friends. She doesn't know if she will marry him. She has her children to consider. But she is thinking about it as she listens to the trains pass.

The play was beautifully written and became one of two short plays broadcast on the BBC's Africa Service which, because it is syndicated across the whole continent, has an audience of about 50 million. Not bad for a first play by a first-time writer.

5

Narrators

In the theatre, the device of having somebody standing on stage acting as a narrator can appear clumsy or even redundant unless very skilfully used (as it is in Tennessee Williams' *The Glass Menagerie* or Brian Friel's *Dancing at Lughnasa*). Voice-overs in film or television drama need to be used very sparingly, as do scenes in which people explain things to camera. There's always a danger that the storyteller will come between us and the story being told.

Radio, on the other hand, thrives on narrators. Of course, it's perfectly possible to write a radio play without any form of storyteller, but it's part of the intimacy of radio that we warm to somebody who has a good story to tell and we are drawn into the interior world of a character whose thoughts and feelings we can share – without, of course, necessarily approving of them.

Sometimes in a dramatisation, the narrator is an omniscient figure, representing the author of the original book, watching and describing the characters. At the opposite end, a radio monologue – in which there is only one speaking character – can also be powerful and engrossing (*Spoonface Steinberg* by Lee Hall is a well-known example) because there is someone talking to us directly in the same way as a friend might. But you don't need to limit yourself to a single narrator: there can be several, with different viewpoints and different things to tell us about the experiences dramatised in the play.

We've chosen some examples to illustrate some of the options available to you.

The first is a clever and witty variation on the author as omniscient narrator. It's the opening of Part Two of *Matilda* by Roald Dahl, dramatised for radio by award-winning playwright Charlotte Jones. First broadcast in 2009 in the Radio 4 Classic Serial slot, it was produced by Claire Grove. Charlotte Jones has invented a playful narrator who, though very much in the spirit of Roald Dahl, is a wholly original character. Played by Lenny Henry, he has an overview of the characters and he can also interact with them, but he is not always in control of them.

Example One

From *Matilda* by Roald Dahl, dramatised by Charlotte Jones

PART TWO: SCENE ONE

FX:	SPRIGHTLY MUSIC.
NARRATOR:	(V.O.) *Oh you're back are you? How long's it been? A week? Mmm. Seems like longer. Still, you want to know what will happen to Matilda? Fair enough. She's a beguiling child, if I say so myself. So. Where were we, before we were so rudely interrupted? Ah yes, the setting is Matilda's infant school – Crunchem Primary. It is Wednesday and tomorrow the reception class will be inspected by the Headmistress. Cue Matilda's greatest adversary – that hammer-throwing, fire-spitting virago of a woman – Miss Trunchbull.*
FX:	DINOSAUR FOOTSTEPS APPROACHING.
NARRATOR:	(V.O.) *Hold your horses! Not so fast, lady. Let's take this step by step.*

FX:	THE FOOTSTEPS STOP SUDDENLY.
NARRATOR:	(V.O.) *Matilda and her classmates must prepare for their headmistress to arrive. The readiness is all. So I must hand you over to Matilda's sweet and delectable class teacher – Miss Honey.*
FX:	INTERIOR CLASSROOM. CHILDREN CHATTERING.
MISS HONEY:	I have some important news for you, children, so listen carefully. You too, Matilda. Put your book down and pay attention.
NARRATOR:	(V.O.) *Matilda you will remember is a genius and is following her own course of study. What is it you're reading now, Matilda?*
MATILDA:	(V.O.) *The decline and fall of the Roman Empire.*
NARRATOR:	(V.O.) *Ay, caramba! And only five and three quarter years old.*

The second example is from *The Kneebone Cadillac* by Carl Grose, an Afternoon Drama first broadcast in September 2011 and produced by Claire. Carl Grose has written extensively for Kneehigh Theatre Company and this was his second play for radio.

The Kneebones are a bunch of Cornish desperadoes who live hard lives, drive weird vehicles and love country and western music. The narrator, Maddy Kneebone, is the central character in the drama. We see all the action from her point of view so we live the story with and through her. But her voice can also whip us through backstory and get us quickly from one location to another.

Example Two

From *The Kneebone Cadillac* by Carl Grose

<u>SCENE 1</u>	**<u>EXTERIOR. UNITED DOWNS RACEWAY – DAY</u>**
<u>FX:</u>	<u>AN EPIC SOUNDSCAPE OF CAR ENGINES AND PUMPING MUSIC DROWNED OUT BY A VAST, CHEERING CROWD.</u>
TANNOY:	…and as you can see all the vehicles are on their marks, revved up and rarin' to go! Judgin' by some of the awesome cars on display, I think we can expect to see some pretty spectacular action this afternoon! And remember, folks: the louder the cheer, the bigger the crash!
<u>FX:</u>	<u>AN ALMIGHTY CHEER GOES UP.</u>
TANNOY:	Ideal! Drivers stand by…

<u>INTERIOR. CADILLAC – CONTINUOUS</u>

MADDY:	(V.O.) *My name is Maddy Kneebone. I'm eighteen years old and I live in St Day which is sorta between Redruth and Chacewater in case yer wonderin'. I got two brothers and a cat called Elvis. I'm tellin' you all this cus I might not survive the next 'alf hour.*
<u>FX:</u>	<u>SHE TURNS THE KEY. HER SOUPED-UP CAR ENGINE ROARS TO LIFE.</u>
MADDY:	(V.O.) *Word of warnin'. You'd best buckle up. It's gonna git messy.*
TANNOY:	And 'ere we go in five… four… three… two… one –

NARRATORS

FX:	NEEDLE LANDS ON RECORD. 'YOU'LL NEVER GET OUTTA THIS WORLD ALIVE' BY HANK WILLIAMS PLAYS.
SCENE 2	**INT. KNEEBONE HOUSE. NIGHT. ONE WEEK AGO...**
SLICK:	Whadda ya playin' that for?
MADDY:	(V.O.) *Thass Slick. 'E's the eldest.*
DWIGHT:	Father wants 'ank Williams on.
MADDY:	(V.O.) *Thass me middle brother, Dwight.*
SLICK:	'Ere. I'll choose the track.
DWIGHT:	'E asked me to do it, Slick.
SLICK:	Yeh but you dunt know.
DWIGHT:	I dunno what?
SLICK:	What 'is fav'rite track is.
DWIGHT:	Course I do. I'm playin' it now, aren't I?
SLICK:	That ain't 'is fav'rite track, ya plank. And 'tis 'ardly appropriate now, is it? Mind out the way.
DWIGHT:	Get off.
SLICK:	Budge over, Dwight!
FX:	THEY TUSSLE.
SLICK:	Stop bein' so damn childish!
DWIGHT:	S'the old man's dyin' wish, Slick.
FX:	THE VOLUME ON THE SONG GETS TURNED UP.

SLICK:	You stubborn little –
FX:	<u>THE TUSSLE ESCALATES INTO FULL-BLOWN FIGHT. ELVIS THE CAT FLEES IN HORROR.</u>
MADDY:	(QUIET) Slick?
DWIGHT:	Sod off, y'pillock!
SLICK:	I shall 'it you in a minute!
MADDY:	Slick.
SLICK:	What?
MADDY:	'E's gone.
FX:	<u>SLICK AND DWIGHT CRASH INTO THE RECORD PLAYER. THE NEEDLE IS KNOCKED OUT OF ITS GROOVE WITH AN AMPLIFIED BUMP AND SCRATCH!</u>
SLICK:	Daddy's dead?
MADDY:	Yeh.
DWIGHT:	Great. 'E didn't even get to 'ear 'is fav'rite toon!
SLICK:	Cus you're a stubborn prat, thass why! Right. Upstairs. All of us.
MADDY:	(V.O.) *Father 'ad bin ill for some months so when Slick called me to finish work early and get 'ome quick, I knew this was prob'ly it. Time I got there, the boys 'ad already bin upstairs to make their peace. Dad died while I was with 'im. I could tell Slick wadn't too 'appy about that.*

Our third example is from an unusual and inventive monologue by Hattie Naylor called *Ivan and the Dogs*, an
Afternoon Drama first broadcast in 2009, produced by Pier
Productions and directed by Paul Dodgson. It won the Peter
Tinniswood Award for Best Play on Radio in 2010 and subsequently went on to become a stage play which was
nominated for an Olivier Award in 2011.

Of all the true stories that came out of Russia during the
period of perestroika, this is one of the strangest. Four-year-
old Ivan Mishukov walked out of his drunken parents' flat
and went to live on the streets of Moscow, where he was
adopted by a pack of wild dogs. When the play begins, Ivan
is eleven and he is telling the story to a foster-mother who
has promised him a dog.

The story is told solely from Ivan's point of view. In the
opening we hear Ivan's drunken parents in the background,
but their dialogue is in Russian and is treated like a sound
effect; the parents themselves don't carry any of the narrative. The rhythms of Hattie Naylor's stark, bleak play have
the steady simplicity of a child's speech.

Example Three

From *Ivan and the Dogs* by Hattie Naylor

SCENE 1

IVAN: So. All the money went and there was
nothing to buy food with. Mothers and
fathers couldn't feed their children or their
animals. Mothers and fathers tried all sorts
of things to find money, to buy food, but
there wasn't any because all the money was
gone. So mothers and fathers tried to find
things they could get rid of, things that ate,

things that drank or things that needed to be kept warm. They looked about their flats for these things.

The dogs went first.

They took them in their cars and drove them to the other side of the city and left them there.

But still there was no money, so mothers and fathers looked for other things, other things that ate, and drank and needed to be kept warm and children were taken to the other side of the city and left there.

You have promised me a dog, Erina, if I tell you my story. I have been with you for three years now. Now I'm eleven, then I was four.

So, I can't remember everything because I was very little but I will tell you as much as I can.

I will tell you as if it's now. Dogs live like it's now. And this is now.

FX:	BACKGROUND: INTERIOR FLAT. A LARGE MAN FALLING ON THE FLOOR AND GETTING UP.
WOMAN:	(IN RUSSIAN) But I…
MAN:	(IN RUSSIAN) Get off. Where have you put it, you bitch? Where have you put the drink.
FX:	MAN STUMBLES BACK UP.
MAN:	Get off me I don't need your help.
IVAN:	(V.O.) *And this is my mother and my stepfather.*

FX:	BACKGROUND: INTERIOR FLAT. A LARGE MAN FALLING ON THE FLOOR AND GETTING UP.
MAN:	(IN RUSSIAN) Did you drink it?
IVAN:	No.
WOMAN:	(IN RUSSIAN) Don't hit him.
MAN:	(IN RUSSIAN) Why is he here. All he does is eat and drink.
WOMAN:	(IN RUSSIAN) No Kolya. No Kolya.
MAN:	(IN RUSSIAN) Out of my way.
FX:	THUD. SCREAMING. MOTHER AND FATHER FIGHT. IVAN SCREAMS 'NO'.
IVAN:	(V.O.) *He has fists like for ever, like hammers, and he builds red mountains across my skin.*
FX:	SCREAMING CONTINUES.
WOMAN:	(IN RUSSIAN) No Kolya. No Kolya.
MAN:	(IN RUSSIAN) Out of my way.
FX:	THUD. SCREAMING. MOTHER AND FATHER FIGHT. IVAN SCREAMS 'NO'. LATER THEY CURL UP TOGETHER ON THE FLOOR.
IVAN:	(V.O.) *Every night is like this.*
FX:	THUD. SCREAMING. MOTHER AND FATHER FIGHT. IVAN SCREAMS 'NO'.
IVAN:	(V.O.) *In the morning he will beg her to forgive him and promise on his mother's life*

	that he will never hit her again. And she will say it's because we have nothing. She'll say it's because he has not been paid for months, that it's because the bosses steal – and then she will blame the boss of everybody, who is called President Yeltsin. And then she will cry and he will cry, and she will tell him that he has a soft heart.
FX:	OPENING OF DOOR.
IVAN:	(V.O.) *And then she will kiss his red face all over. And he'll promise again on his mother's life that he'll never hit her again. But he's lying.*
	His mother should have died many times.
	But now is tonight, they are curled up on the kitchen floor – holding hands with nothing. It is May and the ice on the river has just broken. So I go.

Our final example is from *Witness* by highly experienced, award-winning radio writer, Nick Warburton. It is the story of the Prodigal Son from a five-part dramatisation of St Luke's Gospel, broadcast every afternoon in the week before Easter 2009. The producer was Jonquil Panting. *Witness* won the 2009 Sandford St Martin Award for programmes which explore religious themes.

As well as using multiple narrators, the script creates a fluid relation between story and narration. The characters are telling the story, and then the story begins to be enacted around them and they take on the roles of the characters they're describing: for example, Peter becomes the Prodigal Son. And we manage to be in two places at once; we are round a table telling a story and then, simultaneously, we're on a hillside. This is something wonderfully unique to radio.

Note that the writer uses 'narrating' in the stage directions rather than voice-over (V.O.). This is perfectly acceptable because it is absolutely clear what the actors are expected to do and what the text should sound like.

Example Four

From *Witness* by Nick Warburton

FX:	LAUGHTER AT THE MEAL IN ZACCHAEUS' HOUSE. SEVERAL PEOPLE IN A CLOSE ROOM.
JUDAS:	(NARRATING) So we went to the little tax collector's house, and he gave us food. And the Master talked about…
JESUS:	Losing and finding. You know what it's like.
FX:	THE TALK AND LAUGHTER SETTLES AT THIS. THEY ALL LISTEN.
JESUS:	How it is when you've lost something and you find it again, and you're more glad than you were before.
PETER:	If you do find it.
FX:	A LITTLE LAUGHTER…
JESUS:	Yes, if you do. Our Father feels that joy – and more – if he finds one of you again, after you've been lost.
JUDAS:	(NARRATING) 'There was a man,' he said…

JESUS:	A farmer, and he had two sons, and the younger one said to him, 'I'll get a share of everything you have, won't I?'
PETER:	(NARRATING) So why do I have to wait?
JUDAS:	(NARRATING) He was the younger one.
PETER:	(NARRATING) Why can't I have it now?
JUDAS:	(TO JESUS) He shouldn't have asked. He shamed his father by doing that.
JESUS:	All the same his father split everything up and shared it out between the two lads. And soon the young one was off, taking the lot, and going abroad...
PETER:	(NARRATING) For a good time...
JUDAS:	(NARRATING) Which means a wild time, which means forget about the work in hand. Which means squandering his inheritance.
PETER:	(NARRATING) So the money went...
JUDAS:	(NARRATING) Of course it did.
JESUS:	Everything. And then it went from bad to worse. The money was gone and there was nothing to eat, so he got a job looking after pigs. He watched them feed and he wished he could join them at the trough, share in their swill...
PETER:	(NARRATING) But he couldn't. He had nothing...
FX:	PETER IS NOW IN THE ROOM WITH JESUS AND HE SHARES IN THE TELLING.
PETER:	And there was no help.

JESUS: Then he said to himself...

PETER: My father's got servants and they all eat.
                They eat and I starve.

FX: SLOWLY CHEAT OUT THE SOUND OF
                THE ROOM. WE'RE MOVING
                IMPERCEPTIBLY INTO THE WORLD OF
                THE STORY.

JESUS: (NARRATING) So he thought he'd go home
                and see his father and plead with him.

PETER: I'll ask him to forgive me. Tell him I've
                wronged him and offended God. And it's
                true. I have and I'm fit to be no son of his.

JESUS: Maybe he'd take him on, not as a son but as
                one of his workers. So he set off, back to his
                father.

FX: BRIEF MUSIC TAKES US TO A BLEAK
                ROAD WITH A WIND BLOWING.

JESUS: Now every day this lad was away, his father
                would leave the farmhouse and go out the
                front and up to the top of the rise. He'd stand
                there a while and look down the long track
                where he'd seen him once disappear.
                Nothing there.

JUDAS: So every day he'd take the lonely walk back
                to the house.

JESUS: Then, at last...

JUDAS: Far, far down the track...

JESUS: Someone was making his way...

JUDAS: And he knew...

JESUS:	(QUIETLY) Oh, my son…
JUDAS:	He was making his way home.
JESUS:	My son!
FX:	HE BEGINS TO RUN.
JUDAS:	He ran all the way down the hill, and flung his arms round him…
FX:	JESUS AND PETER CLASP EACH OTHER. THEY'RE BOTH OVERCOME.
JESUS:	My son, my son!
PETER:	Father!
JUDAS:	And he kissed him. (COLD) He kissed him. (BEAT)
JESUS:	You've come back. My son…
PETER:	(UPSET) Don't call me that. I don't deserve it…
JESUS:	You are. My son, come home to me.
JUDAS:	He got fresh clothes for the lad and ordered one of the men on the farm to slaughter a calf. They were going to celebrate.
JESUS:	I thought you were dead. I thought I'd lost you…
JUDAS:	(NARRATING) And they went back to the house together.
FX:	THEY WALK DOWN THE ROAD TOGETHER. MUSIC TAKES US TO THE YARD OUTSIDE THE FARMHOUSE. BEHIND THE CLOSED DOOR CAN BE HEARD LAUGHTER AND SINGING.

JUDAS: The other son, the older one, was working in the fields at the time. So when he got home and he heard voices in the house, and singing…

What's going on?

JESUS: One of the men told him. His brother had come home. He was back, safe and sound. They were celebrating.

JUDAS: Celebrating? Celebrating what?

JESUS: (NARRATING) So he stayed in the yard. Wouldn't go in, wouldn't have anything to do with it.

FX: A BURST OF LAUGHTER FROM THE FARMHOUSE AS THE DOOR IS OPENED.

JESUS: Son?

JUDAS: I'm all right.

FX: THE DOOR IS SHUT ON THE CELEBRATION.

JESUS: Why don't you come in?

JUDAS: Come in? For what?

JESUS: Didn't you hear? Your brother's…

JUDAS: I heard.

JESUS: Then…?

JUDAS: He's back. I never left.

JESUS: No, but…

JUDAS: I stayed and I worked. I worked and worked, year after year. You put on a party for me, did you? Ever? Listen to them in there.

JESUS: Because your brother's come home...

JUDAS: He took your money and he threw it all away. Drink, women, who knows what? And it all gets forgotten.

JESUS: Can't you be glad? I love you the same as him.

(JUDAS IS DISMISSIVE)

No, listen. I gave him up for dead and here he is with us now, alive and well. Won't you be happy with us?

(NO RESPONSE)

Won't you come inside? It's why I came out here. To find you, and to bring you in.

(PAUSE)

JUDAS: (NARRATING) I didn't answer. I looked across the table. Jesus, Peter, the others. And the little tax collector, intent on every word.

Over to You Again

If you've heard any radio plays recently which used narrators, then why not take a look through your radio-drama diary notes (yes, that again) and see how effective you found the way they were used. You may well be surprised how often narrators of one sort or another are employed.

And now is an opportunity for you to try to write something for a narrator of your own. For the moment, keep it simple and create a short monologue. Write ten or twelve lines, a few hundred words, no more.

You might like to base it on somebody you know. Or a character from a book or television series you're very familiar with. Or you might want to create a character from scratch.

The objective is to see if you can catch your character's voice and get him or her talking convincingly. And get us wanting to know what happens next.

6

Heard Not Seen

Words and sounds are all we have on radio. Well, music, of course, but that's simply a rarefied form of sound. And everything you write into a radio script must translate into sound and words or else it's redundant.

In Part Two we're going to start looking at what creating drama in sound effects and words means in practice, but we want to end this opening survey of the potential of radio drama by giving you some examples of imaginative radio writing at its best. There's no need to read them all right away. They repay careful study and hopefully you'll find them inspiring.

Extract One

Love Contract by Mike Bartlett is an Afternoon Drama first heard on Radio 4 in 2007 and produced by Claire Grove. Mike turned it into a stage play a year later at the Royal Court under the new title *Contractions*. Since then it has been performed all over the world. It was also nominated for the Peter Tinniswood Award for Best Radio Play and the Theatre Management Association Award for Best New Stage Play.

It is a dark, futuristic comedy told through a series of increasingly bizarre interviews between Emma and her manager. Emma has secretly begun a relationship with a man in her office, which breaches a clause in her contract. Her manager says she will be dismissed without a reference, her credit rating wrecked, and even her child may be taken from her. Inspired by an article Mike saw in the *Guardian* about a number of companies asking staff to declare office love affairs 'to guard against jealousy, favouritism and break-up fallout', this play is *The Office* meets old-style Eastern Europe.

What's particularly interesting about it as an example of radio writing is that it breaks the usual conventions. There are no voice-overs to explain or editorialise and there's a very minimal use of establishing sound effects at the start. It's stripped down to two voices in conversation.

From *Love Contract* by Mike Bartlett

SCENE 1

FX:	THE SOUND OF A LIFT RISING. THE DOORS OPEN. EMMA STEPS OUT.
MANAGER:	Emma.
FX:	THE DOORS CLOSE.
MANAGER:	Come in.
	Sit down.
	How are you?
EMMA:	Fine.
MANAGER:	Good. Good.
EMMA:	How are you?
MANAGER:	Oh me. I'm fine too. Thank you for asking.
	Thank you for asking Emma.
	And how are things at work?
EMMA:	They're good. Thanks.
MANAGER:	Tell me.

EMMA: I'm settling in well. My sales figures started average and have been improving. Yes. I think it's all going very well. Thanks.

MANAGER: Good. And the office?

EMMA: The office?

MANAGER: The office. You get on with everyone?

EMMA: I think so.

MANAGER: No problems? No arguments?

EMMA: No.

MANAGER: Disagreements?

EMMA: About what?

MANAGER: Anything.

EMMA: Well there have been... I mean I have disagreed with some views. About sales. About our approach.

MANAGER: You have.

EMMA: Yes. It's part of my job. We all express our opinions. You know.

MANAGER: And then you come to some kind of consensus...

EMMA: Yes.

MANAGER: And the work continues down that agreed route...

EMMA: Yes.

MANAGER: You have disagreements with others in the office. But they are resolved amicably.

EMMA: Amicably yes.

MANAGER:	So you are all friends?
EMMA:	No. I wouldn't call them all friends. But we get on.
MANAGER:	I see.
	Well that all sounds… fine.
	Emma?
EMMA:	Yes?
MANAGER:	I want to remind you of something.
	This is the contract you signed when you joined the company.
EMMA:	Yeah.
MANAGER:	Sorry?
EMMA:	Yes.
MANAGER:	Did you read it? Before you signed it?
EMMA:	Yes.
MANAGER:	Good. Have a look at page three will you? Paragraph five.
EMMA:	Okay.
MANAGER:	Does it start 'No employee, officer or director…'?
EMMA:	'No employee, officer or director'. Yes.
MANAGER:	Can you read it please?
	Can you read it out loud please? So we can discuss it.
EMMA:	Oh.
	'No employee, officer or director of the company shall engage with any other

employee, officer or director of the company in any relationship, activity or act which is wholly, predominantly or partly of a nature which could be characterised as sexual or romantic, without notifying the company of said relationship, activity or act.'

MANAGER: Do you remember that paragraph?

EMMA: Yes.

MANAGER: You read it?

EMMA: Yes. I think… Yes. I did.

MANAGER: Good.

It exists to safeguard against unfair or discriminatory conduct.

To insure against favouritism.

EMMA: Sorry. I don't understand.

MANAGER: I wanted to draw it to your attention.

EMMA: Why?

MANAGER: In case you had forgotten to read it.

EMMA: What made you think I had?

MANAGER: We all miss parts of contracts sometimes.

EMMA: So this is just normal practice? You remind everyone?

MANAGER: Oh.

Everyone?

No.

EMMA: Why me then? Are you implying… something?

MANAGER:	No.
EMMA:	Are you implying that I am having a romantic or sexual relationship with someone else in the company?
MANAGER:	No.
	Because you would tell me if you were, wouldn't you?
EMMA:	Yes.
MANAGER:	Good.
EMMA:	Sorry... Obviously I don't understand.
MANAGER:	I think you do. You've read it over. Out loud. We both heard you. So that's alright now. It's all very clear. Isn't it?
EMMA:	Okay.
	Yes.
MANAGER:	Good.
	Would you like to take this opportunity to talk to me about anything else?
EMMA:	No.
MANAGER:	Good. Well that's all then. Thank you.

Extract Two

49 Donkeys Hanged is a sixty-minute drama by Carl Grose, written for Radio 3's The Wire in 2008 and produced by Claire Grove. A Cornish writer, Carl was performing with Cornish theatre company Kneehigh in Soweto. Heading back toward central Johannesburg, he saw a headline in a local newspaper: '49 Donkeys Hanged'. The newspaper reported that a farmer called Solomon Singo had hanged forty-nine donkeys from the branches of trees on his land. Why would a man do such a thing? And (merely on the practical level) *how* could a man do such a thing? Good questions, Carl thought, for the starting point of a drama.

And the drama he came up with is a wildly imaginative dark comedy that plays with reality. It opens with a massive storm and the voice of Cornish farmer Stanley Bray narrating in the present while he prepares to hang a donkey in the past. Stanley is compelled to hang donkeys. He does not know why. His wife Joy, who is in a wheelchair, is desperate to get out of the house. Stanley has boarded up the windows. Their way of life is fast disappearing, the farm is bankrupt and this is Stanley's bizarre response.

It's pure radio. The dialogue in the opening is minimal. The atmosphere and narrative are invoked almost entirely through sound effects. This outstanding piece of writing is full of exciting production challenges, not least of which is what does a donkey being hanged sound like?

From *49 Donkeys Hanged* by Carl Grose

SCENE 1	**EXT. BOSANKO FARM. NIGHT**
FX:	RUMBLE OF THUNDER. AN OLD TRUCK APPROACHES. CLATTERS UP THE DRIVE. BRAKES SQUEAL TO A HALT. DOOR OPENS. BOOTS LAND HEAVY IN A PUDDLE OF MUD. WE FOLLOW THEM ROUND. TWO BOLTS ARE DRAWN BACK. A TRAILER DOOR COMES DOWN WITH A SHRIEK AND A CRASH!
BRAY:	(V.O.) *So. Wanna knaw how to 'ang a dunkey?*
FX:	FROM WITHIN, A DONKEY HEE-HAWS.

BRAY: (V.O.) *This way.*

FX: <u>A SECOND OMINOUS RUMBLE…</u>
      <u>HOOVES CLATTER UNSTEADILY DOWN</u>
      <u>THE METAL RAMP AND ONTO</u>
      <u>CONCRETE. THEY WALK.</u>

BRAY: (V.O.) *I seen the beast from 'cross the valley,*
      stood shakin' in ole Weezer Jenkins' field. 'E
      bin there years. Nuthin but skin an' bone.
      Nice'n light, I thought, so 'ere we are.
      Weezer barely looked up from his paper.
      'Take'n off me 'ands, Stanley. Saves me
      shootin the damn thing.' A cold-hearted
      bastard is Weezer.

BRAY: (TO DONKEY, HARD) Stand there.

FX: <u>HAMMERING ON METAL.</u>

BRAY: (V.O.) *I rigged the tree up earlier. Sink this*
      iron spike in the ground, got summin to tie'n
      off with…

FX: <u>THUNDER. CLOSER, LOUDER.</u>

BRAY: (TO DONKEY) S'get this over yer head.

BRAY: (V.O.) *Tied the noose meself. 'ope she 'olds.*

BRAY: (TO DONKEY) Looks like rain any minute…
      Right. 'Ere we go!

FX: <u>BRAY HAULS THE DONKEY – THE</u>
      <u>EFFORT IS IMMENSE.</u>

      <u>THE DONKEY CHOKES AND SNORTS</u>
      <u>AND WHEEZES. CLOAKING THESE</u>
      <u>SOUNDS SOMEWHAT, THE THUNDER</u>
      <u>CRACKS AND BOOMS!</u>

BRAY:	(WITH EACH HAUL) Go on...! Hup...! Geddup there...! Ya BASTARD...! GYAHHH...!
<u>FX:</u>	<u>THE ANIMAL EVENTUALLY DIES. BRAY IS BREATHLESS. RAIN POURS DOWN.</u>
BRAY:	(V.O.) *Thass one. Only another forty-eight to go.*

Extract Three

The Loop by Nick Perry is an Afternoon Drama first broadcast on Radio 4 in 2009 and produced by Toby Swift. It was Nick's first play for radio and it won a Bronze Sony Radio Academy Award in 2010. Nick has subsequently written two more Afternoon Dramas, and an original fifteen-minute drama series, and has adapted a noir thriller for late-night Radio 4.

In the play, set primarily in the present, a four-year-old boy called Zack toys with his dad's mobile phone and his father, an English writer called Nick, finds himself speaking to a stranger called Jim in New York – in 1959! Jim is writing for the cult American television series, *The Twilight Zone*. Jim thinks if they work together they can make money from this bizarre time warp but Nick wants to use their gift for the greater good. The idea for the play came from Nick Perry's young son, who used to dial long strings of numbers when his father wasn't paying attention, which resulted in, among other things, a call from Twickenham police, as in the script.

The drama plays with time throughout. Again, it's a piece which could only work in radio. The characters and their relationships are totally credible, but fact and fiction are cleverly interwoven and the world around them is often on the move.

Our extract begins about four minutes into the play...

From *The Loop* by Nick Perry

JAKE:	(TO PHONE) Hello?... Is my mummy there?
NICK:	Jacob! Who are you talking to? Give me that! (TO PHONE) Hello, sorry, is that Twickenham police?
JIM:	(MALE, AMERICAN ACCENT, REMOTE PHONE PERSPECTIVE.) Twicker-what?
NICK:	Is that... Sorry, is that...?
JIM:	This is Lexington 7576...
NICK:	Lexington? Is that America?
JIM:	No, small island off the east coast called Manhattan. How can I help you?
NICK:	Manhattan, oh my God, I'm so sorry, it's my son, he's been... Gosh, it must be the middle of the night there...
JIM:	No, it's... No, it's not the middle of the night, it's... Are you, where are you calling from?
NICK:	From London. London, England. I hope I didn't wake you...
JIM:	No, you didn't wake me, it's ten after three, I'm at the office.
NICK:	It's...?
JIM:	Hey, wait a minute. We've spoken before, right?
NICK:	Uh, I don't think so.
JIM:	I think we have. You sound familiar.
NICK:	Well I'm sure I'd, uh...

JIM: You don't recognise my voice?

NICK: Not really, no.

JIM: Okay then. My mistake. But hey this is a great wire, I mean for an intercontinental call, it's very uh…

NICK: Well yeah, I, uh, and I'm on my mobile…

JIM: Your mobile what?

NICK: My mobile phone.

JIM: Your mobile phone, what's that?

NICK: That?… It's my, oh right, you call it a cell, I'm on my cellphone.

JIM: Your cellphone? So you're in jail and there's a phone in your cell?

NICK: (FORCES A LAUGH) Yeah, yeah, that's right.

JIM: Really?

NICK: No, not really. I'm on my cell. My cellphone.

JIM: Cellphone? No, I never heard of it.

NICK: You live in New York City and you never heard of a cellphone?

JIM: No, sir. Actually I live in Jersey, I just happen to have an office in the city.

NICK: And you never heard of a cellphone.

JIM: No sir.

NICK: What're you, Amish?

JIM: What's Amish?

NICK: Amish, you know, like in the… like in that Harrison Ford movie… um, oh.

JIM: Harrison who?

NICK: *Witness!* That's the one. What do you mean, Harrison who? You know the one where they… there's that famous scene where they're putting up the barn, the barn-raising scene… they're Amish, the people with the, with the, you know… bonnets.

JIM: I have absolutely no idea what you're talking about.

NICK: Oh come on. Luke Skywalker. Indiana Jones. He's one of the most famous people on the planet…

JIM: Who is?

NICK: Harrison Ford!

JIM: Not to me. Maybe in England.

NICK: Okay, you never heard of Harrison Ford, you work in an office in New York City, what do you do for a living – what's your name?

JIM: James. Jim.

NICK: What do you do for a living, James Jim?

JIM: I'm a screenwriter.

NICK: A screenwriter?

JIM: Yeah.

NICK: (BEAT) And how's that going?

JIM: Pretty good, as a matter of fact. Yeah, okay, you know.

NICK: Because do you know what the really weird thing is, James Jim? Apart from the fact that you're possibly the only living screenwriter who's never heard of Harrison Ford?

JIM: No, what?

NICK: I'm a screenwriter too.

Then – a little later in the same scene – Nick discovers that the mysterious American claims to be calling from a different time zone in a different era –

NICK: Okay, okay, wait a minute, if it's 1959 where you are...

JIM: What do you mean, where I am? It's 1959 all over the world!

NICK: Okay, no, wait, I've got an idea... your name is Jim what?

JIM: Giller.

NICK: Jim Giller. Gee i double-ell ee. Ar?

JIM: Yes.

FX: SOUND OF KEYBOARD TAPPING.

NICK: Okay, and you're working on *The Twilight Zone* and what was that other one you mentioned, *Science Fiction Theatre*...

JIM: What're you doing?

NICK: I'm googling you.

JIM: You're what?

NICK:	Just bear with me. Okay, this is weird, this is so, so weird, my friend... Jim Giller born 1930 Yonkers, New York...
JIM:	Hey.
NICK:	... is that you?
JIM:	How'd you know that about me? Who are you?
NICK:	That's mad. That's just mad. You're on Wikipedia my friend. You wrote twelve episodes of *Science Fiction Theatre*...
FX:	SOUND OF MOUSE CLICKS.
JIM:	Is this the FBI?
NICK:	Do I sound like the FBI?
JIM:	Then how in hell do you know –
FX:	SOUND OF JIM'S VOICE SUDDENLY BECOMES DISTORTED AND HIS WORDS INDISTINCT, CLIPPED, SUCKED DOWN INTO A SPIRALLING ECHO.
NICK:	Jim, you there? Jim?

Extract Four

The Diva in Me by Charlotte Jones started life as a one-woman stage play written for actress Philippa Stanton. Charlotte adapted it for radio and it was broadcast as an Afternoon Drama in 2011, produced by Claire Grove.

It tells the story of Phil, a woman with an astonishingly versatile voice – and Philippa Stanton really can sing like almost anyone, from Björk to Shirley Bassey! In the play, Phil is looking back on her life. How did someone with so much talent end up eating toast alone on a Saturday night?

The version for radio is essentially a musical for an actress and a pianist. A bold stylistic choice. The principal difference between the stage play and the radio version is that, on radio, Charlotte used other voices for Phil's family and friends whereas, on stage, Philippa played all the parts. We decided that what was a wonderful virtuoso turn on stage wouldn't work anything like as well on radio, where the listener needs more help to follow who is who. The radio version also had to be about half the length of the stage play, a difficult job that required reshaping the narrative while allowing the music sufficient time to breathe.

With *The Diva in Me*, Charlotte created a big, funny, moving story in a concise and stylish form. She keeps the story moving at a brisk pace and Phil's narration guides us from one location to another. In radio drama, unlike in most other dramatic forms, a scene can take place in lots of locations, switching line by line or even taking place in several locations simultaneously. And Phil's musical impersonations worked especially well on radio: she practically *becomes* Sinead O'Connor, Shirley Bassey or Edith Piaf because we can't see her.

The extract that follows is from about ten minutes into the play.

From *The Diva in Me* by Charlotte Jones

SCENE 5

PHIL: (V.O.) *Trouble with me, I'm a late developer. I don't get over the five foot mark till I am twenty-one. I routinely stuff cotton wool in my training bra. The possibility of a boyfriend in my life is very very slim. But aged sixteen by some miracle I meet Dill from Daventry. We meet at the Daventry Dog Show.*

FX:	<u>DOGS YAPPING. DOG-SHOW NOISES IN THE BACKGROUND. SIT! STAY!</u>
COMMENTATOR:	And next in the ring we have Suky Stephens and her Afghan Silky. Look at her go. What a bitch!
FX:	<u>A RIPPLE OF APPLAUSE.</u>
PHIL:	(V.O.) *Dill has a dachshund called Dave.*
DILL:	Dave! Dave! Sit. Stay. Bad dog, Dave. Dave, leave the lurcher alone. Oh! You're showing me up, Dave.
PHIL:	(V.O.) *Dill and Dave come bottom of their show class. Sweet, dappy Dill, named after the herb! I am the same age as JUDY was when she made* Wizard of Oz *and Dill is my SCARECROW. How I love him. He is sweet and funny with long hippy hair and a winning smile. The thing you should know at this point is the main reason Dill is rubbish at the Daventry Dog Show is because Dill has no right arm and Dave the dachshund is small but lively.*
FX:	<u>DAVE THE DACHSHUND GIVES A CHIRPY BARK.</u>
PHIL:	(V.O.) *Instead of a lower arm Dill has a hook on a prosthetic limb.*
DILL:	I have to oil it once a week. It's no bother.
PHIL:	(V.O.) *When I introduce Dill to my parents, the hook sends them into a spin. Don't get me wrong, my mum and dad champion Dill.*
TREVOR:	He's a great kid, that Dill.

MONA:	Very brave.
PHIL:	(V.O.) *They love him all the more for his disability. But it makes them nervous.*
FX:	CHINESE MUSIC.
PHIL:	(V.O.) *One night Dad takes us all to The Oriental Palace. My dad loves a Chinese.*
DILL:	I've never had a Chinese before, Mr Stanton.
TREVOR:	Oh Dill, you haven't lived son! I can highly recommend the duck in black bean sauce. Tangy without being too hot.
PHIL:	(V.O.) *My dad is showing off to Dill, trying to win his favour. But he has forgotten about one thing. The chopsticks. Chopsticks and the hook are a recipe for only one thing: humiliation.*
FX:	EATING. CHOPSTICKS.
DILL:	Can't seem to get the hang of this.
MONA:	Oh dear, Dill. Oh God love him. Let me wipe your shirt down. What if you put your napkin up top? Do you want a hand with that? When I say a hand – I don't mean – Oh dear.
PHIL:	Shut up, Mum.
TREVOR:	I'm sure we can ask for a spoon.
DILL:	You're all right. I'm not that hungry anyway.
PHIL:	(V.O.) *The chopsticks are too much for brave Dill. Our relationship flounders over the chop suey. I am heartbroken. That night back at*

The Chesford House Hotel, my dad knows he has done wrong.

FX: <u>HE SPEAKS INTO THE WALKIE-TALKIE.</u>

TREVOR: Nipper One? Do you read me? Plenty more fish in the sea, Nipper One. Nipper One? You're a good kid, our kid. You know that?

PHIL: (V.O.) *I am sad, sixteen-year-old sad and I want my dad to understand. But I let my latest diva do all the talking:*

(SINGS AS SINEAD O'CONNOR) *'Since you took your love away.'*

(V.O.) *Of course I soon forget about Dill because at sixteen and a half I get accepted by the National Youth Theatre. I am not the only one. James Bond is there too. Sing it, Shirley!*

(SINGS AS SHIRLEY BASSEY) *'Goldfinger!'*

(V.O.) *None other than Daniel Craig is in my play. Of course he fails to notice me in all my four-foot-eleven divaness. But someone else does. The play is called* Maps for Lost Lovers *and that's where I find him – the man every diva needs. His name is Timothy Wonderwood and he is as gay as the day is long. We call him Shadwell. I don't know why except he is Welsh and a terrible moaner. But he is also magnificent. And the minute he hears me sing, HE KNOWS.*

SHADWELL: Flippin 'eck mouse, that's a beltin' set of pipes you got on you there. You and me we're gonna be tight now. I love a belter, me.

Hopefully we've got you thinking about the huge imaginative potential of radio drama and you've felt encouraged to try some of our exercises to get you thinking about your own potential.

In Part Two, Stephen looks at how you move on to creating your own radio drama.

Thinking in Sound

You're about to create a one-minute radio play with no dialogue at all. All you need is any simple recording device, such as your phone. It's better to do this with someone else so that you've got an extra pair of hands to create sound effects, provide feet for walking, slam doors, grate cheese, etc. Allow a maximum of twenty minutes to plan what you're going to do and about twenty minutes to record it.

First, take a moment to listen to the sounds around you and think about other acoustics that are available in the building you're in or nearby. What story can you tell using sound only? There must be no dialogue, but you can sigh, laugh, whistle, exhale, etc. Your work will be unedited so you need to record your sounds in story order. Be as imaginative as you can. Stairwells can be full of echoing possibilities, kettles exude menace and chopping vegetables close to a microphone can be terrifying. Get your microphone as close to the sounds as possible and see what you can create.

When you've recorded everything, play it back. And there you have it, a one-minute, sound-driven piece of radio drama. It's even better if you can play it back to someone who was not present when it was made. What do they think they are hearing? What story do they think you are telling?

To finish, try writing one line of dialogue to add to the soundscape that you've created. Just see what it suggests. Play back the soundscape and read in your line, preferably to someone listening. What do they hear? Where could you take this story next?

Claire did this exercise with some writers in Johannesburg. Two of them went to the basement car park of the large tower block that they were working in. One walked through the echoing underground labyrinth whistling, while the other one drove a car towards them at speed. There was a squeal of breaks, a thud and the car stopped. Silence. The ticking of hot metal. A long pause. Then the whistler started up again and walked away into the distance. Phew! We are not recommending you do anything this dangerous, but it produced one minute of brilliant radio with not a word of dialogue in it.

PART TWO

Creating Your Own Radio Drama

STEPHEN

1

Introduction

If you buy a guidebook to a famous city, you can get a lot of pleasure sitting at home finding out all about it, imagining what it would look like, where you would like to go and what you would like to eat. If you actually take your guidebook on a visit to the city, you use it in a different way because you're physically there in the city. You understand why the guidebook advises this or recommends against that, its maps help you to chart the streets and you discover in a very real way what's it like to be there.

Similarly, a book about radio drama can hopefully help you to an understanding of how radio plays work, but it's only when you actually start trying to write your own play that you really understand what it's like. In this and the following sections of this book, we look at ways of helping you with the process of creating and writing (and rewriting) a radio play, and then move beyond to take you all the way through the submission and production processes.

Although we will be looking later on at writing comedy, drama documentary and radio dramatisations, in Part Two we will be concentrating mainly on the BBC's Afternoon Drama. There are more slots available on radio for the Afternoon Drama than any other and realistically it's the only slot which is readily available to first-time radio writers. (Although, of course, because it's an interesting form, experienced writers return to it again and again.)

This is why we recommend that you start by aiming to complete an Afternoon Drama. It can come in many shapes and many styles, as you've hopefully discovered from your listening and the notes you've kept. But there is one clear limiting factor. An Afternoon Drama lasts forty-five minutes, no more and no less. Which, in practical terms, is about 8,000 words, including all character names and all stage directions. (The familiar screenplay convention of a page per minute is less helpful because, on radio, a page of monologue or narration will often play at a much slower speed than a page of short, sharp dialogue exchanges.)

Dealing with the practical limitations can, of course, be daunting. But it can also be helpful. Because a novel can be any length, novelists can struggle for years to find a length and shape for the material they're creating. And there is no such thing as the correct length for a stage play or for a screenplay either. But knowing that you have to write something of a particular length will hopefully help you to focus on what you want to say.

So let's begin the process of creating an Afternoon Drama.

Note: The examples of bad radio writing in Part Two have been written specially by Stephen for the purposes of illustration. No other radio writer is involved.

2

The Germ of an Idea

So where do ideas come from? I've always enjoyed the response given by the late Douglas Adams to a fan who asked him where he got his ideas from. He answered that he got them from a small mail-order firm in Dorking. Or words to that effect.

The process of finding an idea which we like and believe in, which we are prepared to live with throughout the demanding process of writing a play and beyond, is obviously in a large part intuitive. My fantastic idea might not inspire you to want to develop it, and vice versa. It's tied in to who we are and what we're interested in.

Oh, and would it work as a forty-five minute radio play?

When I was running an online course on radio drama, at a certain point I always asked the writers involved to come up with an idea in just a sentence or so which they would like to work on. On one occasion, one of the writers came up with this idea –

'Two gay penguins in the zoo adopt an egg.'

Personally, I loved this idea, which was, I think, inspired by a newspaper story. It was a quirky and potentially very funny take on the controversial subject of gay adoption which wouldn't get bogged down in soap-opera-type realism. It was an idea that could only work in radio – or possibly in cartoon form, but even then everything would still have to be far too visually concrete for the idea to really take off. It had a clarity and simplicity which meant that the story could probably be told in forty-five minutes. I could

CREATING YOUR OWN RADIO DRAMA

already imagine the zoo world – keepers and animals – and how they might comment and gossip. And I for one wanted to know how gay penguins talked to each other. Indeed, how they'd become gay penguins in the first place. Many of the other writers on the course were equally enthusiastic.

But the writer who offered the idea disappeared from the course. Either he wasn't that interested in his idea or he didn't know how to take it any further. Possibly he panicked when he realised how difficult it was going to be to write this piece. I have no way of knowing and no blame should be attached to his decision, given how demanding the process of developing the idea would be. After all, there are other things to do in life. I just wish I'd had that idea.

But it does show there are two significant factors in choosing an idea. One is whether or not it has the potential to work in radio terms and appeal to listeners and to potential producers. The other is whether you do or don't want to go the distance with the idea you've chosen.

All of us are different and the subconscious process that delivers an idea which intrigues us enough to want to live with it and develop it is different for each of us. Some writers draw very directly on personal experience. It's interesting that one thing that immediately comes across in an idea when it's presented is whether the writer knows what he/she is talking about. If you've trained as a singer then drawing on your own experience will illuminate, say, a play about a great singer like Caruso or a play about singing in the church choir. If you've worked in a garden centre then you know things about different types of plant and the sort of customers who buy them that most people don't know. If you understand the principles behind the Higgs boson then there's almost certainly a drama to be made out of it. But only if you understand – and are inspired by – the physics, and the people.

We all hold in our heads experiences nobody else has had in quite the same way as we have. It could be being mugged at the bus stop. It could be skydiving in Scotland. Or stacking shelves in the local supermarket.

But the idea may not be based on direct experience. It could come from history or today's newspaper or a story a friend tells you.

As it happens, one of my most personal radio plays, *Memorials to the Missing,* came from a trip on Eurostar with a group of friends, and the subject was not in any way based on my own direct experience. We went and had lunch in Arras in France, and after lunch we visited the English War Memorial there designed by Sir Edwin Lutyens. On a beautiful sunny day, there was this tranquil green space filled with gravestones, all apparently identical from a distance. When you looked closely, there was information about the rank and the religion of each of the dead soldiers – so they were given individuality and also presented as part of the same experience. One of my friends was an expert and I asked him who had been behind this very imaginative scheme. He explained to me about Fabian Ware and his creation from his own personal initiative of the Imperial War Graves Commission. The information lodged in my brain and some time later surfaced in a proposal for an Afternoon Drama. My fellow contributor, Claire, read the proposal and later (a long time later) admitted to me that she'd read the summary and thought it was going to be the driest, most boring play she could imagine. She wasn't scheduled to produce it, I should add. It was directed by that doyen of radio producers, Martin Jenkins, for the Brighton-based independent company, Pier Productions. And somehow as we worked on it, the documentary aspects of the story became transformed by the presence of the voices of dead soldiers, wanting their stories to be told. It became about how voices from the past are heard and how powerful is the wish we all have to be remembered. Because it was radio, the dead could speak. Their voices were as urgent as those of the people who were alive, and whether or not the living could hear them was an important part of the drama. The result made people cry. I hadn't expected that or planned it. Indeed, if I'd calculated on that happening, then it wouldn't have happened. (An extract from *Memorials to the Missing* can be found in Appendix 2.)

The point of this story is that there is no right or wrong way to find an idea which inspires you. In this case, I thought it was an interesting (and frankly sellable) subject because very few people knew the story of how the war memorials had come into being. But it turned into something about loss and the wish to be remembered that struck a powerful chord in me, and then in many other listeners.

I hope I'm not making the process of choosing your subject harder rather than easier. But there is no magic formula. There is only your own instinct about what you really care about.

Starting Off

Write down any ideas you have for a radio play.

At this point, don't self-censor. Put down whatever interests you.

Remember this is a story told in voice and sounds, and it can last no longer than forty-five minutes.

Do not leave any idea out because it seems silly, clichéd, or difficult to write.

Write down all the ideas you have.

Do not throw any of them out. Yet.

And don't worry just now if they're not clearly expressed or fully developed.

The growth of an idea

Ideas lodge in your brain, you write them down and perhaps that's all that happens to them. But sometimes they'll linger, you'll return to them, you'll mentally revise them and they'll grow. You may want to rewrite and expand them.

Sometimes an idea can linger there for years before you know what to do with it. Sometimes it never comes to any sort of fruition and stays in the files. Sometimes an idea will hit you and you'll immediately want to go on to the next stage.

Consciously or unconsciously, ideas reshape themselves.

So what makes an idea start to grow? Let's look a little at this process. If you jot down, for example:

'A family goes on holiday to a haunted house,'

It's a very generalised, almost clichéd idea, unlikely to capture anybody's imagination. It starts to become a bit more interesting if you say:

'A vicar and his family go on holiday to a haunted house,'

Or:

'A committed atheist and his family go on holiday to a haunted house,'

because anybody can see there is potential conflict between the beliefs of the vicar – or the atheist – and a house apparently inhabited by ghosts. How are they going to reconcile the supernatural with their own belief systems? But I would say we're still a long way off something that's original or striking. So let's keep going –

'A vicar and his wife take their adolescent daughter on holiday to a house which she comes to believe is haunted.'

We're still not out of stock horror-film territory, but you can at least see the conflict deepening and becoming sharper. 'The family' has become one very specific child who 'comes to believe' the house is haunted. So are there really ghosts or not? Is the adolescent daughter using this as a way of hinting at her hidden emotional troubles? Or maybe she's deliberately winding up her father because of his religious beliefs. Or maybe there really is a ghostly threat out there? The original statement said 'a haunted house'; now ambiguity about whether it is or isn't haunted enters the concept.

So how is this developing as an idea specifically for a radio play? What are the advantages of this story being heard rather than seen? Are there any obvious benefits?

Well, my instinct is that there are considerable advantages to a radio version. The status of what the daughter does or doesn't see remains ambiguous. A visual medium would have to decide what to show or not to show about what she sees or doesn't see in the house. In radio, her words and the surrounding sounds and voices can draw us into her subjective world. We don't have to make any immediate decisions about whether what she is experiencing is objectively true. Radio can suggest with sound where film or television would have to be more specific. Nor do we necessarily have to privilege her viewpoint over those of her parents, which could be equally valid.

Still, as it stands, the idea is pretty simple, with three characters and a clear conflict, which could be explored within forty-five minutes. Indeed, it might run out of steam very quickly if extended much longer without introducing a number of extra complications.

But there are still questions to be settled. What's the relationship between the vicar and his wife? What sort of house is this haunted house? Is it a creaking ancestral mansion available unexpectedly as a holiday let? Or an ordinary seaside bungalow rented out on a regular basis? Personally, I think the latter's more interesting and unexpected. But then what are the alleged ghosts? Are we talking ancestral feuds, or something unpleasant that happened to a recent holidaymaking family? Or are they ghosts the daughter's brought with her?

The one thing we don't need to know at this stage is whether we do or don't believe the daughter, and whether there are or are not ghosts. That's what you'd write the play to find out.

I am not, of course, recommending that you submit this idea to the BBC. It still doesn't have enough originality or bite. But hopefully it helps you to think about how ideas can expand or change as you put the flesh on the bones. Each concrete decision you make brings further clarity to the idea – and hopefully makes you want to explore it further.

Flesh on the Bones

Here are a couple of basic starting points along the same lines as my earlier example:

'A woman gets an unexpected job offer.'

'A man becomes suspicious of his new neighbours.'

'Two lovers meet up unexpectedly at a party.'

Try to see if you can build any of these into something more promising and intriguing. In particular, see if you can find an angle that calls for treatment specifically in radio. But don't overload the idea with details, and try to keep it to one or two sentences.

The wood and the trees

So far we've been looking at putting flesh on the bones. But often the problem is the other way round: you have huge amounts of material and it's becoming extraordinarily difficult to see the wood for the trees. Or, to stick with the metaphor, find the bones and muscle beneath the mountains of promising flesh.

So how do you get to the core of what you want to do?

We've all heard about the Hollywood film 'pitch'. You refine and refine your idea until you can tell a high-ranking film executive exactly what it is and why it will appeal to him (or, very rarely, her) in about thirty seconds. 'It's *Top Gun* meets *The Full Monty* set in Tokyo' or whatever. From the outside, if you don't need that movie job, it's very easy to ridicule this approach, but I've come to think that if you can't explain your basic idea for a radio play in a few very clear and economical sentences then you're not really sure what it is you're intending to write about.

Somebody asks you what your play's supposed to be about and you find yourself saying, 'Well, it's about this man who wants to climb a mountain because – well, it's complicated – you see his wife has been seeing another man. She's a schoolteacher and so's her lover, but the man who wants to climb the mountain, he works for an insurance company and there's a crisis because the company may be about to be taken over by – well, by the lover's older brother, who's also a mountain climber, only he wants to climb the mountain for a different reason, to do with his guilt about his mother's death and anyway – did I explain about the pupil who has a crush on the man's wife?'

These are the words of somebody who is full of ideas but isn't clear what the core of his or her radio play is going to be.

At this point, it may be helpful to look again at your radio-drama diary, where, hopefully, you've been keeping notes on the plays you've been listening to. Did you find it hard to summarise the content of a particular play you'd heard? The chances are that you did. Frankly, nobody finds this sort of summary easy. It's very difficult not to get over-involved in the detail, and then find you're telling the story moment by moment rather than conveying its essence.

Hopefully, if you persisted, the task got easier. And trying to do it for other writers' work can help to bring clarity to your own ideas. Remember, we're looking for the core of an idea, the thing that makes you want to start writing.

Describing the Story

Look over the entries you've made in your radio-drama diary. Alternatively, just search your memory bank for plays you've listened to recently.

Select a couple of the plays which you enjoyed and which have stayed with you in your imagination.

Take a look at what you've written about them. Does it really convey the essential quality of what you heard? If you had to explain to somebody else what the play was about, do you think what you've written does the job properly?

If not, have another try. You've just heard this fantastic radio play. You want to write to your friend and describe what it was about.

You've a hundred words to do it in.

If you find the exercise helpful, try it with more than one play.

The road ahead

We've been looking at ways in which we find and express ideas.

One thing I hope has emerged is that a forty-five-minute radio play needs a strong central idea. This is not the slot for a sprawling family saga covering five generations. Or a chronicle of the entire life of a long-lived famous poet. Or a complicated cross and double-cross spy saga set across three continents with a cast of thousands.

So here's a paradox. You have to dig through all the ideas in your head and try to find the one you really care about. Then you have to find the core of what you want to do and express it as simply and clearly as possible. And then know that it will expand, get complicated and end up probably not where you expected it to end up. But that's one of the basic reasons why we write. To find out what's going to happen.

Ready, Steady

Look at the ideas you have. Is one of them burning a hole in your pocket? Do you think it might be ready to go?

Write it up now in no more than three sentences, no more than one hundred words.

We're not holding you to this. Inevitably your ideas will change and develop. But we both, from our different perspectives, think it's very useful at this point to have on record what you think the radio play you're going to write is about.

3

Getting Started

So when are you ready to start writing?

How long is a piece of string?

The only answer is that you're ready whenever an idea in your mind has reached the point at which you feel the need to start exploring it on paper or on the computer screen. Which probably means you have started asking yourself questions about what's going to happen next. Or you want to know about the characters you described. Or you've realised there is a way through that huge collection of ideas you've been living with for months.

Let's look at some of the questions you need to be asking.

Whose story is it?

Well, of course, it's about more than one person because that's the nature of drama. Even a monologue needs to contain conflict and dramatic interaction.

And, of course, it's perfectly possible to write a piece for two voices where neither is privileged and we have no access to the internal thought processes of either character.

But in the Afternoon Drama slot there's only forty-five minutes to tell the tale and most of us struggle to find a focus for the story we want to tell within those limitations. To return momentarily to the haunted house idea as it was starting to develop in the previous chapter: there are three characters – the vicar, his wife and their adolescent daughter.

All are important, each has a different perspective. The vicar faces a conflict between his beliefs and his daughter's claims about what she has experienced. The daughter is allowing herself to be obsessed by ghostly voices which she may or may not want to explain to her parents. And the mother, so far the least explored character, is trying to make sense of her daughter and her husband, and of the conflict between them. Maybe she is in crisis herself – are there other children? Is she losing her own faith? What's her background? Why did she marry her husband? And so on.

There are no right answers to these questions. All three characters are important but, to be frank, it would be extraordinarily difficult to give their voices equal weight within the confines of forty-five minutes. Somebody's needs have to drive this story, whether it has a narrator or not.

Some years ago, I wrote a play called *Party Animal* (an extract can be found in Appendix 2). It was about a scandal involving a boy who died in mysterious circumstances at a celebrity party with a male host and predominantly male guest list. There were important questions I needed to answer: was the boy gay? Was he a prostitute? How did he die? But the first question I needed to settle was: whose story is this?

Well, it could have been the story of the boy's mother. She could be a single parent involved in a search for the truth. It could have been the story of the celebrity host who's involved in a frantic cover-up to save his reputation, and may or may not be directly involved in what's happened at his party. Or the story could have been told by the boy himself and, because this is a radio play, he could be talking to us directly and it might only gradually dawn on us that he is dead.

But I had an instinct that the focus should be the boy's father. At the same time, I was stuck because I didn't know enough about him. Then I realised the solution: the parents were divorced and the son had bonded with his mother, leaving the father ignorant of his lifestyle. So the father's journey was not just about finding out the truth but it was also a journey about finding out something about the son he was emotionally and physically separated from. His motivation to tell us the story was stronger than that of any of the other characters. Or so it seemed to me. But I still hadn't found the father's voice.

And then I talked to somebody at my local gym. His circumstances were very different from my character, though he was divorced and living with a new partner. He told me about his business. He owned a couple of railway arches and his firm made sandwich fillings which were sold all over London to sandwich bars offering ready-made sandwiches. Vast amounts of egg mayonnaise was being created every day in a railway arch just round the corner from my house. On one level, this had absolutely no relevance at all to the story I had to tell. On another level, this knowledge allowed me to start writing. The man started to speak to me and the more he spoke, the clearer it became that this was above all his story.

Voices and the characters associated with them will always be battling for your attention. But I think it's a reasonable guiding principle to ask yourself – who needs to tell his or her story most? Who has the most to find out, the most to tell, the most to explain and excuse, the longest emotional journey to travel?

So – is one of the characters talking into your ear and insisting that you tell the story from his or her point of view?

The other voices may still be important, but once you've found that core narrative, they become easier to understand. They're there to dramatise and focus the central figure's journey and ultimately they can't be allowed to hijack it for their own ends.

This leads to a second question –

How are you going to tell this story?

In order to start writing, you don't need to know how your play is going to end but, obviously, you do need to know how it's going to start.

You've identified the core of your story, but there are other parts of your approach you still need to think about. This is a play that, however many people are listening, is fundamentally going to be delivered to an audience of one. You have to bear that in mind.

Ask yourself, for example, are you going for a first-person narrator who tells their own story?

Just to repeat – there's no need for a single narrator if it's not right for your story. There can be multiple narrators. There can simply be dialogue without any narrative voice at all. But the question of the central focus of your play still remains, and thinking about your use of a narrator is perhaps the clearest way to start doing that.

If you are going to have a narrator, say a middle-aged woman, is she telling this story to anyone in particular? For example, she could be talking to the police, or to a lover, or to her child. All these choices affect the tone of what's being said and would give the narrative voice a particularity and intimacy that a more impersonal storyteller narrator would lack.

Is she telling this story for any particular reason? Does she feel guilty about something she's done wrong? Has something terrible/wonderful happened and she needs to apologise or explain? Is she in shock or does she want to tell us why her life turned out the way it has? As a general rule, the stronger the reason for needing to talk, the stronger the narrative thrust of the play.

But when we talk of somebody narrating the story because they 'need to talk', we're not thinking of somebody just telling us what happened. The story needs to be fully dramatised. The more it moves into scenes which show our narrator in contact and perhaps conflict with other people the better. The old maxim 'Show, don't tell' applies to radio drama as much as any other form of fiction. If our narrator has a crucial row with her boss, we need to hear it. If thieves break into her house while she is at home and in bed then we need to experience the immediacy of her disbelief and the terror as she confronts the burglars. Just telling us how scary it was won't do.

And just a reminder, we've been talking as if your potential narrator and your characters all have to be human beings. Because this is radio, that doesn't have to be the case. Remember the gay penguins. Your narrator could be an animal or a bird or a motor car or a wooden bench. Or your narrator could be the sort of person who imagines his pet, motor car or fireplace to be communicating with him.

I once wrote an Afternoon Drama about the story of how the Elgin Marbles were bought for the nation in the early nineteenth century. To be honest, I was feeling a bit at sea because, although the subject was undoubtedly interesting and the historical figures involved were fascinating, I couldn't find a central focus for the story. Choosing one of the main figures as narrator somehow didn't seem right as I couldn't see which of them should be privileged in that way. Finally, I had a breakthrough. Why not make the narrator one of the Marbles themselves? After all, what happened to them was at the core of the story. It also reminded the listener that here was something with a far longer history than any of the human participants. It also gave me an opportunity to refer to the continuing controversy over whether the Marbles should be returned to Greece. So I went to the British Museum, looked at the Marbles and selected one of the most dramatic of the fragments on display – South Metope XXVII, since you ask. It shows a centaur – half-man, half-horse – in a life-or-death struggle with a human warrior.

And here's how the Marble, as narrator, spoke:

CENTAUR: (V.O.) *For two and a half thousand years I've been waiting for the final blow. Suspended in time, my head is being pulled back as I try desperately to escape slaughter. I'm pressing my hand to a wound I've already sustained in my back while my naked killer, a cloak draped round his shoulders, is grabbing me by the throat with his left arm and raising his right arm to strike me again. But the blow of his sword will never come.* (PAUSE) *And now his head is gone and my head is gone and my kicking horse-like right foreleg is missing and so is his muscular sword arm. We are just a fragment of what we once were.*

FX: THE MURMUR OF THE VISITORS IN THE MUSEUM.

CENTAUR: (V.O.) *Long ago we were part of a proud marble building which gleamed in the sunlight on a hill above Athens. Now we live in a museum and we are known as –*

FX: THE EXCITED BUZZ OF A GROUP OF SCHOOLCHILDREN. THEN THE VOICE OF A HARASSED FEMALE TEACHER.

TEACHER: South Metope XXVII.

So don't close the door on your crazier ideas too soon. They may hold the key to unlocking your problems. Gordon Lea, in his 1926 handbook on radio drama, wrote that if you want to set your play in the heart of a buttercup then the imagination of the hearer will provide the setting. And that's still true, even though the heart of a buttercup sounds perhaps a bit precious in the twenty-first century.

Why, for example, can't your laptop speak for itself?

At what point in the story do you start?

There's absolutely nothing wrong with starting a play with the announcement that 'Today is going to be the happiest day of my life' and then proceeding chronologically through that day. Somehow every listener would know that this day is *not* going to be the happiest day of the narrator's life and is being invited to find out why. And if we learn as we go along that this narrator is very self-satisfied or very naive, the process could be very entertaining and even surprising. It could even end up being the happiest day of the narrator's life for reasons other than the expected ones.

Complicated flashbacks and movements backwards and for-wards in time are far from essential to a radio play. They can even be a hindrance if they became a way of evading the main issues of the play instead of illuminating them. There is no point in artiness for the sake of it.

All the same, the decision still has to be made – at what point in the story are you going to start your play?

Again, there is no right or wrong answer. I once did an adaptation of a short novel by E.F. Benson called *The Blot-ting Book*. The narrator in my version was the respectable family solicitor who apparently unfolded the story of a mur-der mystery in dry, fairly circumstantial detail. It was only at the end of the play that it became clear that the solicitor was himself the murderer and that this dry, circumstantial narrative was in fact his confession as he lay dying on Brighton beach, having consumed a large quantity of poi-son. Another play set in the seventeenth century, *Agnes Beaumont By Herself*, began with the heroine, Agnes, about to face trial for murdering her father, looking back to the circumstances that had led to the trial, and ending up back in the present with her acquittal. (Interestingly, though I thought she was transparently innocent, a number of listen-ers believed her guilty as charged.)

Both of these plays involve retrospection, but in one case the reason is transparent, while in the other it isn't clear until the very end.

You can start at the beginning of your story, the middle or the end. Each of these carries its own momentum.

You know some things about your story and you write to find out the rest.

The First 500 Words

Write the opening two to three minutes of the play you've been thinking about.

That's around 500 words, including stage directions and character names.

Remember what we looked at in the Part One, Chapter Four about ear-catching openings.

Don't worry about what's going to happen next. Just concentrate on finding a way to engage the listener and give a flavour of your idea.

We're not going to hold you to this opening. There's a long way to go.

But you have to start somewhere.

4

Thinking in Sound

In the experience of both of us, one of the things which most worries writers who want to create a radio play is layout. Is there a proper way of doing it? How do you do stage directions? How do you show that it's a new scene? How do you introduce your characters? Will the play fail to please if it doesn't follow the right formula? The anxiety is understandable, but in fact it's less of a problem than most writers imagine.

In Part Four, Claire deals in detail with the subject of what your script should look like. We've also given some examples of layout in an appendix at the end of the book. Hopefully this information will answer your concerns.

The underlying worry is, to be honest, less about getting the layout right than about the fear we all feel (the present writer very much included) when faced with a blank page and the intention to write a radio play.

But there is a very important principle behind some of these worries about layout and I really don't want to undervalue it. In radio, all you have to work with are voices and sound effects. Radio, as we've said, is in your head, not in front of your eyes. So if, for example, you know a character is in his forties and has a strong Birmingham accent, then that's something which will translate into sound and you should describe it. If the disco music that's playing is in the background so your characters don't have to shout at each other when they speak, then that's also worth saying.

Probably the only essential 'technical' terms are 'FX', which indicates a 'sound effect', and 'V.O.', which stands for 'voice-over.' V.O. is a particularly useful term because it helps somebody reading your script to know when the character is addressing the listener directly (or perhaps voicing their private thoughts) as opposed to when they are speaking within a scene and interacting with other people. Voice overs are often recorded separately or in a different acoustic so the sound contrasts with that of the main action. If you're in any doubts, take a look at some of the examples we've given in Part One, Chapter Five: Narrators, or at the script samples in Appendix Two. The crucial thing is that a radio script has to describe as clearly and accurately as possible what the writer wants to be heard. Anything you include that doesn't do that is irrelevant.

What can't be heard can't be seen

Here's a very obvious example of a scene which contains information that simply won't come across on radio:

SCENE: A VERY SMART PUB IN THE CENTRE OF THE CITY

FX: CITY BANKERS ARE GETTING DRUNK AND ONE OF THEM IS DANCING ON A TABLE.

GILLY COMES IN. SHE'S PETITE, EARLY THIRTIES AND WEARING FAR TOO MUCH MAKE-UP. SHE LOOKS AROUND ANXIOUSLY FOR SOMEBODY BUT CAN'T FIND THEM. THEN SHE OPENS HER HANDBAG, TAKES OUT A PHOTOGRAPH. SHE LOOKS AROUND AGAIN. HER EYES CATCH THOSE OF SOMEBODY IN THE FAR CORNER OF THE ROOM.

It's pretty clear that almost none of this information will come across to a listener. The best you could hope for at the start is a loud babble of posh male chatter to suggest the sort of bar it is. Gilly's entrance would simply not register at all, any more than the description of her appearance or her production of the photograph.

If you had to rewrite this scene in radio terms, it might end up something like this:

SCENE: BAR

FX:	A NOISY BAR FILLED WITH CONFIDENT MALE VOICES, LAUGHING AND JOKING.
GILLY:	(MAKING HER WAY THROUGH THE CROWD) Excuse me – excuse me – (LOUDER) Excuse me!
FX:	SHE BUMPS INTO SOMEONE.
GILLY:	Oh, I'm sorry.
BANKER:	What's the rush?
GILLY:	I'm supposed to be meeting somebody here and I'm late and – oh, maybe that's him over there. Excuse me –
FX:	NOISE CONTINUES. SHE CONTINUES THROUGH CROWD.

Here's another example of a scene full of details that won't come across on radio. Have a go at rewriting it yourself. What's the important information here and how can you convey it purely in terms of sound effects?

SCENE: SUBURBAN GARDEN.

FX: MARY, SLIM, TWENTIES, WEARING A SWIMSUIT, SITS IN THE GARDEN IN A DECKCHAIR, SMOKING A CIGARETTE.

IT'S MIDDAY AND THE SUN IS BEATING DOWN. SHE SWATS AWAY THE FLIES WHICH BUZZ AROUND HER. SHE YAWNS. SHE'S NEARLY ASLEEP.

JOSEPH COMES OUT OF THE HOUSE. HE'S LATE-TWENTIES, TATTOOED, WEARING A LED ZEPPELIN T-SHIRT AND HE'S LOOKING GUILTY. HE'S CARRYING A LARGE BIRTHDAY CAKE WITH CANDLES ON IT.

MARY HEARS HIM APPROACHING AND OPENS HER EYES.

JOSEPH: Happy birthday!

MARY: So you did remember!

Over to you.

When you write something, you have to keep asking yourself the question – what are the listeners going to hear? What will they understand from what I give them?

Radio listeners are smart. They don't need everything spelling out. They can understand nuance and they use their imagination to see and understand in their minds what your characters are about. What they cannot do is grasp information that can only be grasped visually. Or pick up details that exist only in stage directions, not in sound.

For the moment, we're concentrating on thinking in sound and how that affects the way in which you start writing your play. If you want to, go back and look at that opening scene of yours. Are you happy with it in radio terms? Is there anything there which wouldn't work in pure sound?

When people worry about layout, they are probably worrying about how to begin, but they are also worrying about the vocabulary of radio. At some level everyone knows 'He's dark with blue eyes and a shaved head' and 'She sits alone in the twilight, lost in her thoughts' are statements which don't work in radio terms. But the discipline of thinking in sound takes time.

And here's another aspect of it. You have voices and you have sound effects and possibly you have music. As we saw in the first part, it's possible to create effective radio drama with nothing but sound. In thinking about how to tell your story, you need to make this work for you. The combination of words and sounds offers a very rich vocabulary.

Same words, different backgrounds

Here's a simple fragment of dialogue between two characters:

MARK: I love you.

JAN: What did you say?

MARK: I love you.

But if we give a specific background to this exchange, our sense of what's going on and who these characters are can change. For example –

FX:	VERY LOUD DISCO MUSIC.
MARK:	I love you.
JAN:	What did you say?
MARK:	I love you.

Or how about this?

FX:	A HOWLING GALE. STORM-TOSSED WAVES.
MARK:	I love you.
JAN:	What did you say?
MARK:	I love you.

Or this?

FX:	THE CLINK OF TEACUPS. TEA BEING POURED. A STRING TRIO PLAYS MUSIC IN THE BACKGROUND.
MARK:	I love you.
JAN:	What did you say?
MARK:	I love you.

The ambient sound, I think, affects our sense of who these people are and what the dialogue is about, even though the words are unchanged. The first example suggests a couple of young lovers bawling at each other in a crowded disco. In the second, perhaps these are two people caught in a storm and the man is trying to make a final desperate declaration of love before it's too late. In the third, the suggested background is so genteel that the woman perhaps has heard the man perfectly well but, in these surroundings, can't quite believe her ears. And don't we somehow almost subliminally believe that the couple in the last example are older than the couple in the disco scene?

So the soundscape can alter how we interpret what's being said. Part of thinking in sound is always to be aware of how you can economically establish a scene or how you can keep the ears of a listener alert by providing a new sound, be it background or foreground.

Same Words, Different Background

Here's another very basic exchange of dialogue:

LESLEY:	Hello, Jake.
JAKE:	Lesley! I wasn't expecting you here.
LESLEY:	I had to see you.

A printing press. Horns honking in a traffic jam. The whirring of helicopter blades.

Try exploring different sound settings for these lines of dialogue and see how their meaning can change as a result. What's the most surprising setting you can find? What's the most clichéd setting? Or perhaps you can even turn a clichéd setting into a surprising one with the addition of a single sound effect?

So far we've thought about how to tell a story in sound, and hopefully the first draft of your opening is on paper or screen. Let's see if we can keep going.

5

Don't Tell Them Everything

Voltaire wrote that the best way to bore a reader is to tell them everything.

The same principle applies to radio drama. After all, you have a real intimacy with your listener; you're not holding forth to a lecture hall full of people. If you think about how you talk to your friends, you will realise that you don't spell out everything, sometimes because they know the people involved and sometimes because you know you'd bore them to death if you told them every single detail of what happened.

It's all too easy to be tempted to explain all about your characters right at the start. The fact that you can use a narrator makes it even easier. For example:

ROS: (V.O.) *I'm facing the most important decision*
                        of my life and I have to decide today. I've
                        been offered a job abroad and I can't decide
                        whether to take it or not. If I do take it, then
                        my mum and dad are going to be very
                        unhappy because they're getting on and
                        they think I should stay here to look after
                        them when they get too old to look after
                        themselves. And then there's my brother and
                        his wife. I don't know whether they're just
                        jealous or whether they resent being
                        lumbered with Mum and Dad when I've done
                        so much of the caring over the last ten

*years. Oh, and I haven't begun to say how
complicated it makes my relationship with
my boyfriend, who works with me but hasn't
been offered the transfer to New Mexico that
I have. We've been together for five years
and maybe if he'd ever proposed to me, I'd
be thinking differently now. This offer has
really put into question the seriousness of
his commitment to the relationship. Not that
the job's without its problems, of course. I've
been doing some research on New
Mexico...*

It's not hard to see what's wrong with this. Not only is there
an overload of information about a large number of people
which is very difficult to grasp, but all the conflicts have
been set out and explained before we've met any of the characters. And Ros has offered us her analysis of their motives
rather than leaving us to discover them for ourselves. Okay,
it could be worse – Ros could tell us right away in the first
sentence that she'd decided to take the job, so even that
question is resolved before we start. But basically, in the version we have, there's simply not enough left for the listener
to want to find out. The writer has half-killed the story in
the opening moments.

A better, if not exactly inspiring, opening might go like this:

ROS: (V.O.) *Today I'm facing the most important
                        decision of my life.*

Then perhaps an introductory scene with the boyfriend (if
she lives with him), which sets up their relationship but keeps
us guessing about what her big decision actually involves.

Or, if she still lives at home with her parents, a breakfast scene with mother talking about hospital appointments and perhaps father downplaying their significance. Again, the question ticking away in the listener's brain is – what exactly is this important decision she's told us about?

But it's not only in opening scenes that it's important not to spell everything out. In radio dramatisations of novels, for example, when there's a lot of story to get through, the listener can sometimes be left with an indigestible lump of plot.

NARRATOR:	(V.O.) *I returned to Wiltshire for the Christmas season but on Christmas Day my father had a fatal heart attack while carving the Christmas turkey. The loss drove my mother to drink and within a matter of months she was consigned to a genteel home for hopeless alcoholics. So it was not until March that I returned to London for the Marchioness's grand ball.*
FX:	CUT TO BALLROOM MUSIC.

Frankly, if this material can't be dramatised, it's better left out entirely. Either this family tragedy matters to the narrator, in which case it has to be given some dramatic weight, or else it hasn't earned its place in the play. Just being told about it gets us nowhere, emotionally or dramatically.

The same principle applies to original plays. It's one thing to drop a passing allusion to something in the character's past that an intelligent listener can pick up on; it's another thing completely to put into narrative something that is really important for the dramatic development of the play. It may seem important to you as the writer but unless it can be made a living part of the play then it's best left in your notes. On the other hand, if you're in any doubt, dramatise the scene anyway, even if you're expecting to cut it. Exchanges, conflicts, flirtations – these can often help us to find out things we ourselves didn't know about our carefully plotted story and its characters. It might even send the story off in a more interesting direction.

Exposition is a problem every dramatist faces. How do you provide the background information about the characters and their circumstances that the audience needs to know? But you mustn't feel you have to reveal everything at once, particularly if it involves writing scenes in which characters tell each other things they know perfectly well for the benefit of the listener. Too much information too early is often not only over-contrived, it is also indigestible. Besides, it cheats the child in all of us who wants to be told a story. Remember how children listen to stories. 'Once upon a time there was a prince.' And then? 'He lived in a great big castle with his mother.' And then? 'He never left the castle.' And then? 'One day he decided he wanted to see the world outside.' And then?

However complex your narrative and however much it moves backwards and forwards in time, the 'And then?' principle always applies. The listener should be kept wanting to know what happens next, where the narrative is going and what the connection between the strange old fisherman back in 1830 and the smart young businesswoman in 2013 really is. Listeners want to be kept listening. It's boring to be told too much too soon.

Time to Revisit Your Opening Scene

Take a deep breath and take another look at that short ear-catching opening you wrote during the Getting Started chapter.

Try reading it aloud. Remember to try to hear it in terms of nothing but voices and sound effects.

What information have you given the listener about your characters and your story?

Does it give away too much too soon?

Does it tell us more than we need to know just yet?

Is there something you could withhold until later in the play? Or maybe something you could omit altogether?

If you were a listener, would it make you want to know more? Does it leave something for later? Does it allow listeners some space for their own imaginations?

Once you've thought about all this, with any luck, you'll be feeling you want to go on.

And then what??

6

Get to the End as Soon as You Can

Just do it. Try as quickly as you can to get to the end of your play. You can always make it better and you will almost certainly have to rewrite it many times, but until you've finished a first draft you can't really begin to understand what your play is going to be about. Or, given the length limit, where your priorities in terms of character and story lie.

As much as you can, follow the 'And then?' principle and keep going. Every line you write and every decision you make about how your characters move forward is helping to define what sort of play yours is and what kind of story it has to tell. You will make discoveries about your characters and your narrative which will remain hidden if you stop halfway or keep going back to the beginning. The only way you'll learn where you're going is by travelling the whole journey.

Of course, we all know this isn't easy. We're all good at making all sorts of excuses. That opening scene isn't quite right and needs polishing just one more time. You just need to do that extra bit of research into where your leading character is likely to go on holiday. And you're not sure if the message in the third scene should come by letter or by phone.

We all employ strategies like this to defer carrying on, but usually it's better to forget about that small point of detail – it's almost certainly not as important as you think it is. *Just keep going.*

And, of course, the time needed for your writing battles continuously with the other demands on your attention. But if

you want to finish your play, you have to make an accommo-
dation with that (and, of course, all the people in your life).

And then?

Undoubtedly, whatever your good intentions and however
disciplined you are, there will come a point when you get
stuck and have no idea how to go on. Staring at the page is
getting you nowhere. The characters have stopped talking
and you have no answer to the 'And then?' question.

At this point the only thing to do is to take the pressure off.
Go for a walk in the park. Or take a long bath. Have an early
night. Whatever is most likely to switch your mind off the
problem for a while.

Because there are two processes going on. The conscious
process in which you work on your project, worry about its
problems, fret over its characters and generally give yourself
a bad time over every little detail. And there's the unconscious process through which somewhere inside you things
are being mulled over without you even being aware of it,
and the project is mysteriously taking shape.

If I'm stuck and go for a walk, it's extraordinary how often a
solution, or at least a couple of useful lines of dialogue, drop
into my head out of nowhere. I never take a notebook, so I
always have to hold on to the idea until I get home. I often
curse myself and think how stupid it is not to have something with me to make notes on. But then if I carried a
notebook, I would be consciously 'working', and there
wouldn't be the same sense of letting go.

Everybody has their own way of taking a break from thinking about what they're writing. There is no right or wrong
way of doing this. Just try and be aware of those moments
when you're feeling that you're beating your head against a
brick wall, and remember that the best thing to do is to stop
making contact with the brick wall and do something else.

[119]

Without exaggeration, I have been very stuck at some point on every single radio play I've ever written (including most of the dramatisations). What I have learned is that you keep going when you can and, when you can't, you take a walk or a bath (or drink a glass or two of wine, maybe) and allow leisure time for the problems to resolve themselves.

Well, there's one other thing I've learned. If you're stuck, it's not usually because of the line you wrote just before you got stuck. It's because of a decision you made earlier. Maybe a character hasn't been developed properly. Maybe there's a point in the story where you've taken a wrong turning in terms of plot or character. Maybe something which needed to be explained hasn't been explained. In which case, all you can do, after your break, is go back over what you've done, re-reading as calmly and alertly as you can, until you find what went wrong. But that understanding doesn't come by constantly reading and re-reading what you've done. It comes from stepping back and giving your mind a break. And *then* going back.

Some Things to Try When You're Stuck
Borrowed by Claire from a generous writer and passed on to many others.

1. The scene in which...

If you are not quite sure what happens next in your play, or what you had planned isn't working, then try this. In two minutes, write as many sentences as you can which begin 'The scene in which...' There's no need to write more than the simplest outline – in effect, a scene title – but each one must be active. For example, 'The scene in which dad discovers his child is missing', 'The scene in which he finds a shoe', 'The scene in which Mum attacks Dad'. Be strict with yourself about the two minutes and write as fast as you can. Don't think too much about it. Let the writing be automatic. Something unexpected just might come.

2. Who gets the next scene?

Ask yourself – if the next scene belonged to one of your characters, which one of them would it be? Pick a character and try writing it. Again, don't think too much about it. Just see where the character takes you.

3. Shift the emphasis

In writing any play or scene you are drawing on a mixture of observation, personal experience and imagination. So if, for example, your play is about two people breaking up, your observed information may come from an aunt and uncle who split up years ago, your emotional information may come from a heterosexual break-up that happened to you recently and your imagination has decided to set your break-up in South Wales between two men. Look at the balance of observation, personal experience and imagination in your play. Are you relying too heavily on one? Is there a way you can shift the emphasis in the scenes that are to come?

4. Something physical...

Another thing you can do is try giving a scene a physical focus. For example, if your characters are discussing something abstract such as God, or death, or a future event, try giving them something physical to grapple with, for example, a cereal bar. Your two characters are arguing about the existence of God but they're also both hungry and there's only one cereal bar. So the theological discussion is interspersed with a tussle over the snack. Introducing a physical focus

CREATING YOUR OWN RADIO DRAMA

like this can give a flagging scene energy and take the play in a new direction.

You can also try this exercise in reverse. Let's say you're writing a scene in which two people tussle about which one of them will bring home the prize pig, i.e. something present and physical. You can insert an abstract notion into it. For example, one character asks the other 'Do you believe in God?' They don't necessarily get an immediate answer. The scene about the pig continues but having fun with the abstract might just open up new possibilities about where the relationship between the characters could go.

Nobody would say it's an easy business to keep on writing until the end. All that can be said is – try to keep going whenever you can and don't beat yourself up too much if you're stuck. Nevertheless, getting to the end is the basic goal.

Letting rip

There's another side to this. We've talked about 'And then?' Sometimes things will start happening in the script that you didn't plan. A character who was supposed to do something decides to do something else. The wedding you'd plotted for your main characters fails to take place. The cousin from Australia turns out to be much nicer than expected and doesn't offend the family in the way you'd imagined. Two characters who were supposed to be having an affair turn out not to like each other very much and drift apart.

Keep calm. Hold on. This is a good sign. The characters are acquiring a life and voice of their own.

Sometimes the sound setting you choose for a scene can also start to change things. You've set your encounter between your two adulterous lovers in a posh restaurant. But the waiter starts saying things you hadn't expected him to say because the setting was just the setting and he wasn't part of the plan. Perhaps he challenges the order by letting them know it's drearily predictable, or perhaps he's in a bad mood and starts to explain why. His intervention may even end up changing the course of the lovers' relationship. Or you move a scene from a busy street to a quiet park, and the dynamic of what's going on is altered by the very different mood generated by birdsong instead of honking cars.

Do not attempt to go back to your original outline and force the characters to comply with it. What is happening is the lifeblood of your play. After all the false starts and careful planning, things are taking off.

Don't self-censor stuff that seems silly to you. Don't worry because things aren't going the way you expected. Every time you can move forward, move forward.

Get to the end in whatever shape you can.

There's a real discipline in getting what you want to say into only 8,000 words. But if you're intensely engaged with what you want to say, it's achievable.

Try to get to the end.

Loosening Up...

So, where are you? If you're in the middle of writing your play, you don't need an exercise. And please don't use this exercise as a diversion from the serious business of finishing a first draft of your play.

But if you need to loosen up or you're feeling totally stuck and can't believe you're ever going to get over it, here's an exercise.

ED:	I'm waiting.
SUE:	What for?
ED:	You.

Choose a setting. Remember we've only got sound to establish where that is.

Choose identities for the two characters. Again, we have only aural information to go on. If you want to make Ed Spanish, that's fine by me.

Finish the scene, however long or however short it is.

The point of this exercise is just to do it. And loosen you up to possibilities.

7

Let It Stew

So you've got to the end of your radio play. Congratulations.

It may be too long and it may seem a bit confused and you're not quite sure exactly what it's about, but you've finished a draft. It really is time to give yourself a break.

Take a proper mental holiday before you go back and have a look at what you've done. Let it stew. Once again, it's time for your unconscious to absorb what's happened and ponder its strengths and weaknesses. This is a part of the process that's not to be rushed.

When you do feel ready, make yourself as comfortable and relaxed as you can and re-read what you've done. Try, if possible, not to start scribbling notes or corrections right away. Try as far as you can to read the script as if it's been written by somebody else. How would you react if somebody sent this piece of work to you? You're never going to become totally detached from what you've written, but you must try and read it with as fresh an eye and as open a mind as you can.

You might try reading it to yourself aloud. That would certainly help you to hear whether the dialogue you've written can actually be spoken aloud by actors. You might notice where the sentences go on too long and you start to lose your breath. Or when you've said something and you don't need to say it again.

You could ask some friends to listen while you read it, or maybe ask some of your friends to read the script and tell you what they think, though a word of warning here: if somebody tells you that something is wrong with your script and makes a suggestion about how to improve it, be cautious and wary. Don't get me wrong, listen carefully. If something isn't working then you need to know. But people are often very free with helpful suggestions – 'Why don't you make him a woman?' 'I think it'd be much better if he was a jazz musician instead of a cellist in an orchestra'. 'I don't like that scene in the cellar filled with rats. It gives me the creeps.'

Do not simply accept their suggestions. It's your play and you mustn't allow other people to rewrite it for you. But, on the other hand, you must pay attention. Sometimes their suggestions are very helpful and solve a problem that's been worrying you. Even if that's not true, if they are feeling concerned about something that 'isn't quite right', then you need to take a look. What you've done may well not be working. So you need to look again, but it's you who must find the answer to the problem, not the helpful friend.

It's very easy to be overwhelmed with all the things that aren't quite working in your play. You need also to absorb what's distinctive and interesting about what you've written. Part of the process is discovering your play's strengths and building on them.

Anyway, you've re-read your play and now you feel you're ready to do some further work.

Here are some ideas which might help you in your assessment of what you've achieved and of what you need to do now.

The original idea

Hopefully you've held on to that short statement you wrote down about what your play is going to be about. Now's the time to take it out and have another look.

There's no doubt that a lot will have changed since you wrote that statement. Maybe you'll think that you've taken your idea a long way and the statement is now pretty much past its sell-by date. So much has happened in terms of character, plot and setting that everything's changed beyond recognition.

But there's another possibility. You find that the original idea had a clarity that you've lost sight of. Too many new characters, too many plot complications, too much chat about things that aren't really central to the story. So you have to ask yourself whether or not there's something important that you knew before you started which will help you now as you work through a rewrite. No hard-and-fast rule here. Maybe there is, maybe there isn't. But it's a good starting point for a rethink.

The length

I've never come across a writer whose radio plays end up too short in the early drafts. It must happen. If you are one of those writers, then you will now have to investigate what needs building up and where your characters aren't developing as fully as they should.

But for the rest of us, cutting back to the lean incisive Afternoon Drama we want to achieve is anything but easy. D.H. Lawrence told us all to kill our darlings, i.e. be especially ruthless with the bits of writing we're most proud of. That's very helpful in encouraging us not to be too precious or possessive, but what if we throw the wrong darling out of the bath along with the bath water?

So let's look at some of the things you can do.

Be kind to yourself. If you've got this far, you've achieved a great deal. This is not just about giving yourself a pat on the back. It's about achieving a relaxation and openness about what might happen next which is creatively useful.

Whose story is it? Part two

In forty-five minutes of radio, not every character can be given prominence all the time. Once again, you have to ask yourself – whose story is the most important? Who has the most burning need to tell the listener what happened to them?

If your work has been going well, more than one of the characters will be developing a life and will of their own. The energy of the play may well have moved to a different character from the one you first identified as the main character. Looking again at the story of the vicar's family in the haunted house, which we first considered in the Part Two, Chapter Two, you may quite reasonably have thought it was the daughter's story. Now you've discovered it's the mother who's the most interesting character. She's losing her faith and she's finding her husband's certainty a sign of rigidity rather than strength. And she's delving into her past to try and discover why her daughter is so unhappy and disaffected. Maybe you've become fascinated by the mother's own past and started writing about her parents and their unhappy marriage. In which case, has the main focus of your story shifted?

But you also have to consider how many characters you need to tell your story. There's no magic rule but it's very easy to have characters in your script who aren't really earning their keep. You might find, for example, that you've created a couple of characters who are there basically as friends to your main character, shoulders for him or her to cry on. Do you need both of these characters? Would it be stronger if you combined them? And maybe if one of them was combined with somebody with a more confrontational attitude towards your main character, the scenes would become more vivid and revealing.

Going back to the haunted house example, maybe the story started with three children because you felt sibling rivalry was also a part of what was going on. Or perhaps Grand-mother had also come along, a further extension of the domestic tension and perhaps a confidante for the adolescent daughter. If these characters are earning their keep in the play by providing an alternative viewpoint and an added source of tension, then by all means keep them. But if the play is overlong and overloaded with complications, think about discarding or combining the minor characters. As a general rule, if you can combine the functions of two characters into one, it can often create a much more interesting (and useful) character.

You need to know all the characters well and that will inform what you write. But they can't all rule the roost. Somebody's preoccupations have to be driving the story forward. With only forty-five minutes, we need to know somebody is in the driving seat. That doesn't mean they're driving well, or even that they know how to drive, but your narrative can't be pulled in the direction of every single character who attracts your attention. Imagine five or six voices standing at a microphone all demanding attention at the same time. The listener's brain couldn't cope.

So once again – see Part Two, Chapter Three – whose story is it?

Some thoughts on exposition

Sometimes it's inevitable that your narrator and/or one of your characters has to explain something to us so that we know enough about the situation and the characters to follow what's going on. We looked at the problem of exposition briefly in Part Two, Chapter Five. Of course, the 'don't tell them everything' rule always applies, but you're still likely to find yourself with some places in your script, particularly near the beginning, where too much is being told to the listener and not enough is actually happening.

If blocks of exposition seem to be sitting undigested in your script, here's a tip about how to solve the logjam. See what happens if you get the next scene in motion before you've finished all the exposition about the backstory of the characters.

Here's a fairly simple example of what I mean from the opening of a dramatisation I did of a short story by W.S. Gilbert called *The Finger of Fate*:

GILBERT:	Today I am going to give you an instance of the desperately strong measures Fate will take in order to bring about an event she has set her mind on.
FX:	THE SOUND OF CONTENTED SNORING.
GILBERT:	(V.O.) *Mr. Frederick Foggerty was a middle-aged bachelor, of staid and careful habits. He was pretty comfortably off, having an independent income of £400 a year and a Civil Service pension of £700 a year.*
FOGGERTY:	(CHILDLIKE IN HIS SLEEP) Hush-a-bye, baby, on the treetop...
GILBERT:	(V.O.) *He was also for many years Secretary of the Warrant Officers' Shirt-frill and Shaving-soap Department, a branch office under the Admiralty, Somerset House.*
FX:	CROSS-FADE TO A CLOCK TICKING. THREE MEN QUIETLY DOZING.
GILBERT:	(V.O.) *Mr Foggerty led a quiet and retired life.*
FIRST FRIEND:	(YAWNING) Is that really the time? Well, well!

SECOND FRIEND: (YAWNING) Doesn't the time fly, eh?

FOGGERTY: (YAWNING) Soon be time for bed.

GILBERT: (V.O.) *He shunned society and associated intimately with the other heads of subordinate departments – but no one else.*

FIRST FRIEND: (YAWNING) It's been a most entertaining evening, Foggerty.

SECOND FRIEND: (YAWNING) Pity it has to end.

FOGGERTY: But then – time flies!

FX: <u>A LOUD YAWN IN TRIPLICATE.</u>

<u>RETURN OF CONTENTED SNORING.</u>

If you can create preliminary aural hints or fragments of the scene you're just about to go into and intercut them with the essential exposition, then the wodge of information will feel much less intimidating and more integral to your story. Here, getting the story moving in counterpoint to the basic explanations about who Mr Foggerty is makes the listener feel the comedy is already under way.

Are you thinking in sound?

Yes, that question is back again when you re-read your script.

Ask yourself – does what I've written work if we're thinking only in terms of voices, sound effects and music?

Put it another way – does this mean anything to a listener? If it doesn't, then it has to go.

It's extraordinarily easy to write a scene in which somebody walks down a corridor and enters a room without thinking through what that comes down to in sound terms.

Or to imagine a scene in which somebody is alone and anxiously puffing on a cigarette without realising that, without context, a listener is not going to be able to make sense of the sounds they hear.

Because we live in a highly visual culture in which we're incessantly bombarded with images, it's often very difficult to blank everything else out and think only about sound. Radio drama is closer to listening to poetry – words, music and sound effects which speak to our brain.

If you're feeling unsure about this, take another look at the examples in the 'Thinking in Sound' chapter of this book.

Is this the right point to start the scene?

This may not seem a very important question but in radio storytelling (particularly with only forty-five minutes available) it's something you need to think about.

For example, if you're writing about a visit, you could choose to start the scene with footsteps up the stairs and a knock on the door. Maybe several knocks to draw somebody's attention. Then the door opens slowly. Then the person inside speaks and asks the visitor's business. He listens and then lets the visitor in. They go through the hall into a sitting room. The host offers a cup of tea. Or a glass of wine. The visitor hesitates and then goes for the glass of wine. The host leaves him alone to his thoughts and then returns. Finally, as he offers the glass of wine, the host says, 'So to what do I owe the honour of this visit?'

In some circumstances, particularly if there's a thriller element to the story, this sequence might work. The caller is on edge, he doesn't know what's going to happen, the host is weird and now he's wondering what the drink is going to be like and whether it's going to be drugged.

In most circumstances, however, you could start with a clink of glasses and the host's words, 'So to what do I owe the honour of this visit?' Any other version of this scene really needs to justify its air time.

So – take a look at your scenes. Do you need the preamble? Can you simply cut to the chase?

Another example of this might be a scene in which a couple are having a picnic. They unpack the picnic hamper and discuss the contents – the exquisite cheeses, the vacuum flask of coffee made from specially selected coffee beans, the elegant salt and pepper set. If the listeners are on tenterhooks about what's going to happen next and they're expecting an emotional explosion, this might be quite effective as a way of building tension. If this is how the listeners first learn about this couple and their rather precious relationship then it could also be very illuminating. If you're halfway through a play and you know these characters very well and the plan is for them to discuss a prenuptial agreement, then let them get on with it. Tell us they're in a park if it's relevant and then go for the essence of the scene.

Never underestimate the intelligence of the radio audience, even though they may be doing the ironing while they're listening. They can make connections. They can pick up a background sound and understand where the setting has moved to. They know when a character's lying because of the way they talk; they don't need it spelled out to them. And if the play's treading water because things are being spelled out that don't need to be spelled out, they'll switch off.

Raising the stakes

It's surprising how often we fail to exploit our ideas as fully or as boldly as we should. We worry about being 'obvious' or 'melodramatic' and end up leaving everything at a much lower emotional level than we should.

When we first start exploring our characters and themes through writing about them, we often make interesting discoveries, sometimes halfway through a scene, but we don't necessarily build on them.

If you want your audience to care about your characters, you have to make them feel there's something important at stake. If a character gets told off mildly by her boss for being late to work, then it's probably not that compelling a scene. But what if her job is at risk and the boss issues a final warning? Or if the two characters had been having an affair and this mild spat uncovers it?

If a character is being teased because they appeared in a television documentary and made a bit of fool of themselves, we ought to ask – should they in fact have made a complete and utter fool of themselves? What's the biggest impact this humiliation could have on their life, their family, their relationships?

Sometimes we feel it's not 'likely' that a character with an important piece of information should knock and enter just when that piece of information is needed. But that's often what strong and compelling storytelling needs. The characters bump into the very person they don't want to meet. The meal he cooks for her isn't just mildly disappointing, it's a culinary disaster. If the dog goes missing, don't necessarily let it be found right away; there may be more mileage in the protracted anxiety of its owners. If the characters take a boat trip, they might get mildly seasick, or they might get caught in a howling gale. Which is going to have the greater impact?

I'm inviting you to think boldly about what you've created in your first draft and to seize the opportunities to make your play bigger, bolder, funnier, more exciting. It really is true that we as writers often get frightened and think – no, I can't do that, it's too much, it's not likely. Give it a try. Raise the stakes.

Cutting

One final consideration, particularly if your play is on the long side – can you say what you have to say with fewer words?

It's common when you're in the recording studio after the actors have read through your play that you suddenly discover that it's too long. There's no magic way of working that out in advance. Just be aware that, at the revision stage, you can sharpen and improve your play by cutting out lines that explain what's already clear. 'I'm tired' or 'I'm feeling very angry with you' or 'Don't you understand why I'm here?' are the sort of trigger lines for something that might be stronger left implicit rather than explicit.

Here's a piece of dialogue which would benefit from the sort of cutting we're talking about.

JUNE: I'm feeling very angry with you because of how you've been treating me today. Do you understand? I don't feel you respect me as a person even though you expect me to wait on you hand and foot. And apart from anything else, you haven't emptied the dishwasher.

How would you shorten this scene? My solution would be:

JUNE: Oh my God, you haven't even emptied the dishwasher.

This is the sort of cutting we should be trying to make as a matter of course. But sometimes the problems are more complex. In Appendix One we give an example of a fairly lengthy dialogue scene which had to be cut by a third because of time considerations. The full scene is printed first. It's 830 words long. Can you cut it down to under 600 words?

The scene as cut by the writer and producer in collaboration is given immediately afterwards for comparison.

And?

Scripts, somebody said, are not written, they are rewritten.

If this is your first attempt at a radio play then you'll have to return to it more than once before it's ready to submit. Frankly, most experienced radio writers understand that as well. You could well be looking at four or five drafts before you feel your play is in shape. That may sound depressing but actually it's often exciting because each time you rework your play its shape and its intention become clearer. Each time you revise, you internalise more and more the nature of your characters and the outline of your story, enabling you to progress more confidently, avoiding the false starts and the dead ends.

It's impossible to predict how many rewrites you'll need to do but it's certainly going to be more than one. And each time you return to your script, the same thoughts apply:

1. Leave time before you do another rewrite. Take time to listen to your own instincts and those of others around you.

2. Are you always thinking in terms of sound?

3. Are you sure what the core of your idea is? Is the right voice at the centre of what you have to say?

4. Do you have the right number of characters to tell your story?

5. Is there anything you want to include but haven't because you think it's embarrassing or silly? It's never too late to let your aural imagination go wild and raise the stakes.

And now I'd like to hand you over to Claire.

PART THREE

How to Get a Commission

CLAIRE

1

Introduction

Radio drama is one of our best-kept national secrets. There is nothing quite like it anywhere else in the world. Every weekday afternoon BBC Radio 4 broadcasts drama to an audience not far short of a million people. This makes theatre audiences look tiny. The BBC is also one of the biggest commissioners of new writing in the world, and writers get to work with producers who are expert at what they're doing. Most BBC producers work on sixteen or more productions a year so they get plenty of chances to hone their skills. One of the things I love about the job is that I am constantly learning new things. Every play is different. Every new production is a challenge.

As a producer it is always a pleasure to introduce new writers to the huge imaginative possibilities of radio drama. It is very much a writer's medium, and writers are in general an interesting and thoughtful bunch of people who rarely turn out to be what I expect. A rip-roaring romance with a Byronic hero and a heroine with all the cunning of a pack of foxes turns out to be written by a tiny, middle-aged woman who works for British Gas. I have no doubt the surprise works both ways!

Producers give good writing a great deal of respect because they know that if the script isn't good enough there is precious little they can do to disguise it. Compared to television the money paid to writers for a radio play is small, but the commissioning process is much simpler and more than twice as fast. And usually the writer only has to deal with one person, the producer, who is also the script editor, director and casting director.

2

Radio Drama Commissioning

The main commissioning round for BBC Radio Drama is in the spring. This is when Radio 4 invites producers to submit proposals for Saturday Dramas, fifteen-minute dramas and Classic Serials. Afternoon Dramas by experienced writers can be commissioned at other times during the year but the majority of those by first-time writers will be bought in the spring. Comedy proposals are also commissioned in the spring. There is a second comedy round in the autumn when the network fills any remaining gaps, but this tends to be for experienced writers only. Proposals for Radio 3's The Wire and Drama on 3 are invited from producers in early summer. Contacting a producer whose work you like can be done at any time but it is easier if you have had a discussion or correspondence in the preceding autumn or winter so you have a working relationship before the spring commissioning round opens.

At the start of each round, Radio 4 and Radio 3 send out a commissioning document to all drama producers. This is written by the Commissioning Editor for Radio Drama and contains the brief for each slot, the timetable for the whole process and up-to-date statistics about who is listening to what. Any producer that you approach, whether they are employed by the BBC or from an independent company, will be familiar with this document. It does not necessarily change radically from one year to another but it contains the banner headlines of what the networks are looking for and examples of drama they have already commissioned. It is an important part of any producer's job to be aware of what the

networks want, what to avoid, the exact dates of the commissioning timetable and how writers' proposals can be best
presented.

Here are some extracts from the 2012 Commissioning
Guidelines with do's and don'ts for the Afternoon Drama
slot. The briefs for all the drama slots contain similar guidance, but the one for the Afternoon Drama is the most
detailed because writers are being encouraged to offer a very
wide range of styles and genres. This information is for producers to pass on to writers, but I think there are some
useful pointers here for everyone.

- Single Drama needs to be singular. It needs to stand
  out.

- Radio 4 is for curious minds. The worst sin you can
  commit is to bore the audience. If it is familiar
  territory, or stock characters where all politicians are
  venal, all journalists immoral trenchcoat wearers, old
  people are decrepit and teenagers misunderstood, it is
  probably a no. We don't want clichés or the familiar.

- What makes the Afternoon Drama is the writer's
  voice. That is what will make today's Afternoon
  Drama different from yesterday's.

- Simplicity is crucial. Many of the stand-out dramas
  have had a cast of six or less. It is hard for the listener
  to hold many more than six characters in their head at
  any one time, and equally difficult for the writer to
  create more than six fresh, original, three-dimensional
  characters in one forty-five-minute storyline.

- We will only commission a very few rites-of-passage
  dramas – given the audience profile, we have a very
  limited appetite for dramas about teenagers coming
  to terms with the world, and we get offered a lot.

- We are keen to commission voices from as many
  different ethnic backgrounds as possible, but beware

of stereotyping: dramas about arranged marriages and/or sons and daughters escaping from their parents, about making the decision to become a suicide bomber, about returning to India/Jamaica/ Poland, dramas about gun and knife crime, or how grim it is to be a foreign worker in a hostile UK are almost the only dramas we get offered. There is a lot more to life and indeed writing dramas than dramatising these all too familiar issues.

• We will favour contemporary stories over period. However, we are still very keen on history and biography, but not bits of history that our audience don't connect with. *The King's Speech* is a very good example – an almost unknown story about King George VI's struggle to overcome his stammer to deliver his coronation speech was a perfect story for the Afternoon Drama long before it was a film. Famous person, someone most of our audience are keen to know more about, but an unknown story. We don't do biopics, we do dramas: simply dramatising someone's life is a non-starter.

Some Things to Avoid

Are there subjects or styles to be wary of, or avoided? Over the years I have frequently been sent plays accompanied by the cheery comment that it is 'perfect for radio because nothing happens'. Please don't do this. If nothing happens the audience will switch off immediately. It can also give the impression that you are rehashing old material without much thought about how it will work on radio. Radio is an art form in itself which most producers are passionate about, so be careful that you don't unwittingly get off to a bad start.

Some subjects do crop up more than others – for example, plays set in the afterlife; plays set in prisons; plays with dead babies in them and cradle-to-grave biographies of famous people. So it's worth being wary of these.

Suicide is another subject to be wary of. Approximately 6,000 people in Britain kill themselves every year. This doesn't mean you can't deal with it, but the subject has to be handled sensitively for an audience that is listening on their own to a network that they trust. Ask yourself, is suicide justifiable and necessary in your drama?

Most producers get sent a great deal of gloomy material. This doesn't mean that every new play has to be resolutely upbeat, but it is important to know why you are plunging us into a trough of despair, if that's where we're going.

But all rules are there to be broken.

> First-time writer Janice Okoh sent me a play that was set in the afterlife, but there was something original about the characters and the shape of the play. It was bursting with energy, but far too well-worn a subject for an Afternoon Drama. I asked Janice to come in for a chat and she had two or three other outstanding ideas. One of them was about a young woman trying to make quick money by marrying a Nigerian to give him EU status. The deal this character was being offered looked relatively simple. What she hadn't considered was that once she moved into an illegal underworld, anything could happen. *A Short Ride to Düsseldorf* was commissioned and Janice has gone on to write radio drama about the oil industry, gun crime and lap-dancing, and she has recently been writing for *EastEnders*, *Casualty* and *Doctors* on a BBC scheme for writers new to television.

Beware of the anniversary. Radio drama is interested in anniversaries, but not exclusively. And if your idea is anniversary-related it is worth remembering that BBC Radio Drama is commissioned at least a year ahead of transmission. If an anniversary is crucial to your idea you need to be preparing your play or pitch eighteen months to two years in advance. It is also worth having a good guess at what anniversary or event-led drama may be coming up. The Olympics, for example, was bound to generate a certain amount of sports-related drama and, at the time of writing, the BBC have already commissioned a large-scale radio drama event for the anniversary of World War 1 in 2014, so they won't be interested in anything else about that subject until 2015 and beyond.

Your Audience: Who is Listening?

There are about 900,000 people listening to radio drama every day. There are slightly more women than men. They are generally over thirty and the largest group of listeners is over fifty. They are smart, well-informed and curious about the world. If you write a drama about the stars, just be aware that some of the audience will have a degree in astronomy; if it is about hospitals, the audience will include doctors, nurses and hospital administrators as well as patients. By and large the audience know what you're talking about. If a play is too simplistic they switch off in droves; if it isn't factually correct, they are quite rightly down on it like a ton of bricks. They are demanding. They want to be imaginatively engaged and they really care about what they are listening to. They are usually listening on their own and they are often doing something else such as driving, cooking, washing up, painting or looking after elderly relatives. They are easily distracted. Radio has the fastest turn-off rate of any drama, and if we don't keep them interested and entertained they rapidly go elsewhere.

So the opening of a radio play is crucial. It has to the hit the ground running and hook the audience with character, situation and story quickly so they know why they are listening. Then it has to keep them guessing what is coming next. Radio dramas are short compared to plays in the theatre. However engaging a bunch of characters is, the audience aren't prepared to wait thirty or forty minutes for something to happen. The writer may know everything there is to know about the characters but it doesn't all have to be spelled out in the play. The audience want to be teased and intrigued. They like putting puzzles together, so the best radio plays are as much about what is left out as what is put in. The highest compliment that any radio writer or producer can receive is when a listener says 'I couldn't get out of the car until I heard the end of your play.' This is music to my ears.

3

Who to Target and How

The main commissioner of radio drama is the BBC. There is some scope for the development of online audio-drama or local radio initiatives – the Resources section at the end of this book lists a few websites that may be of interest if you want to find out more – but at the time of writing these opportunities are not present in any significant or sustained way.

BBC radio drama is produced by independent companies and by in-house BBC producers. The procedure for contacting either of them is the same. All you need is the name of the producer, which you will have in your radio-drama diary, and the name of their company or the BBC production centre where they are based. This information is on air at the end of their programmes, as well as online on the BBC website and in the *Radio Times*. Many of the independent companies are small and only produce their own work, but some are happy to talk to new writers. There is a list of those that are open to this in the Resources section of this book. BBC producers have a slightly larger share of the drama output and the BBC has a specific policy of encouraging new writers, so there may be a slight advantage in trying one of them first, or at the same time as an independent producer. But the most important thing is that you contact someone whose work you've heard and liked, and who you would like to work with in the future. This creates confidence and respect on both sides.

The Secret to Getting a Commission

So what is the secret to getting your script commissioned? It's probably the main reason you are reading this book. You want to know how to get your ideas and scripts made into actual programmes. Well, the secret is this: there is no secret. Most producers and commissioning editors have few pre-conceptions of what they are looking for apart from the obvious: originality, an engaging story about a new subject, or a fresh take on an old one. They want intriguing characters who speak believable dialogue. They are looking for the ability to create a complete imaginative world that is interesting in itself and leaves the audience with something to think about afterwards.

The Radio 4 commissioning guidelines say they want drama to give the listener an 'insight into the way we live now'. This doesn't mean every radio drama has to be about whatever topic is currently in the news. As we saw in the last chapter, this is worth avoiding because, whether it is knife-crime, drug-taking athletes or restorative justice, there will be a stack of plays about these topics already piling up on producers' desks. Being passionate about your idea is very important. If you are passionate about your play then a producer can get passionate too and your script will have a fighting chance. And don't try to give the producer what you think he or she wants. Write what you want to write and you will find that is exactly what every radio producer is looking for.

Standing Out From the Crowd

There is no doubt about it, getting started as a writer in radio is hard. Like all aspects of the entertainment industry, radio drama is overcrowded and incredibly competitive. Ideas are thick on the ground but the talent and application it takes to develop them are less so. So don't despair. Every year Radio 4 commissions over forty dramas in the Afternoon Drama slot by writers who are new to writing for radio. Radio 4 welcomes plays from poets, stage writers, journalists, novelists, short-story writers and complete novices. New, engaging, exciting ways of telling stories is what the Afternoon Drama is all about. So you have an advantage here: untried and untested writers are being actively sought by BBC and independent producers for this slot. All you need is proof that you can write dramatically. This could be an existing drama script or scenes from a drama that you want to write with an accompanying synopsis.

Think about the ideas you want to write, or the play you've written. What is it that uniquely qualifies you to write this play? A story you've heard, a job you did, a poster you saw? Why is it special? What makes you passionate about it? What is special about you? The place you are from, a hobby, a language, an unusual interest? Think about what makes you and your writing stand out from the crowd.

Making Contact with the Producer

Radio 4 and Radio 3 commission drama at least a year ahead of transmission. If you are pitching an idea in the spring of 2014 you will hear whether it has been successful in the summer or early autumn of that year, and your drama will be on air sometime from April 2015. So how do you get ready for this?

It is important to be bold and imaginative when you are getting started as well as being realistic about the fast-paced industry you are trying to get into. There is no single way of getting into radio drama, but here are some of the main routes.

1. Contacting a producer whose work you've heard and liked. You will find addresses and contacts for BBC and independent producers in the Resources section of this book, or you can contact them through your agent if you

have one. There is no particular advantage in contacting a producer via an agent. You don't have to have one at this point and, if you do, an agent specialising in fiction may not know much more about radio drama than you, so it's worth checking how up to date their information is.

In your letter or email to the producer, say why you are targeting them, i.e. what you've heard. You don't have to lavish the production with praise. Be straightforward and brief. I've had quite a few letters from writers along the lines of 'I heard your play about surfing, here is mine.' This isn't a helpful approach because it means the BBC has recently covered the subject and the producer may also want to move on to something fresh.

Make it clear in the letter or email whether your script is a sample of your writing or a radio play that you would like to have commissioned. Let the producer know what you want, e.g. that they read your script and, if they like it, you want to come in and discuss ideas. Also very briefly outline your writing experience or anything related to the play which will make it stand out. For example, that you live in a yurt in Wales and that's where your drama is set. If you haven't heard anything from the producer you contacted within a month then follow it up and check that your script has arrived. Be aware that producers are busy but we're a friendly bunch. Writers are the lifeblood of what we do so most of us will try to be as helpful as we can.

Writer Sebastian Baczkiewicz sent me an interesting theatre play and we got together for a chat. He talked about his work and I talked about what I thought made good radio drama. Six months later a script with a yellow cover landed on my desk. He had written it on spec. It was called *The Prettiest Girl in Texas*, about a fictional brother and sister who risked everything they had to make a fast buck from an encounter with President Kennedy. But it was November 1963 and Kennedy was never going to arrive. The play was commissioned and Sebastian has been working in radio drama ever since. His popular drama *Pilgrim* has had five series commissioned and he dramatised *The Count of Monte Cristo* in four episodes for the Classic Serial.

2. If you have a stage play being put on, a rehearsed reading or even a poetry event, invite the producer whose work you like to come along. Producers like getting out and about. It's an opportunity to meet you and find out about your work. It may just get your script read.

Annamaria Murphy from Cornwall approached me because I knew her poetry – it's all over the walls at the Eden Project – and I had heard her read her short stories. She had a radio idea, a really good one. The play was to be set in a beauty parlour where Rosie, the proprietress, hears the most intimate secrets of the village. As a writer of short stories Annamaria was worried about being able to fill forty-five minutes, so she fused three stories and got her first commission, a beautifully written Afternoon Drama called *Rosie's Beauty*. Other Cornish writers have approached me since because, even though I'm based in London, they know from my work that I have a particular interest in writers from that region.

Is it worth contacting more than one producer at the same time? Two different BBC producers, or a BBC producer and an independent? Yes, I think it is. Drama is subjective and your subject or style may have more appeal for one person than another. And by sending it to more than one producer you are increasing your chances of being read and heard. But it is not useful to send your play out to every producer you can find. Be selective, based on your radio-drama diary, so you know something about who you are writing to. It is also very useful to get the advice of a radio writer, if you know any, or your agent if you have one who is familiar with the radio industry. It is not useful to target two BBC producers in the same region. They will be sharing information with each other about new writers in their area so you are not increasing your chances by swamping the BBC production centre nearest you.

3. BBC Writersroom is another place to start. Send them a script. Their website (www.bbc.co.uk/writersroom) is full of practical information about how and when to do this. The downside is that they receive a huge number of scripts and so going via them can be slow.

> Mike Bartlett, who has subsequently written for the National Theatre, the Royal Court, Paines Plough and for ITV, sent a theatre script to BBC Writersroom. About a year later it was passed to me by a development producer. I thought the writing was outstanding. I met Mike and we pitched a heavily edited version of the play for Radio 3's The Wire. *Not Talking* won best radio play and best newcomer award for that year and I have done numerous radio productions with Mike since. So BBC Writersroom is a slow way in, but it can work.

4. Go in for a competition. BBC Writersroom's website, mentioned above, is a really useful source of information about what is current. The website is constantly updated so it's worth checking regularly.

> Aspiring comedy writer Alex Boardman went in for
> the BBC Writersroom Laugh Track competition. His
> script was one of nine selected out of over 800
> entries. He was invited on a week-long residential
> writing course in Kent. There he met producers from
> television and radio and heads of commissioning as
> well as other writers. He describes it as 'one of the
> best weeks of my life'. Two months later his script was
> one of three chosen to be performed in front of a live
> audience at the Edinburgh Festival. He described the
> experience as 'brutal' but wrote 'I probably learned
> more about writing in Edinburgh at that twenty-five-
> minute performance of my script than I have ever
> done before.'

Preparing Your Script

The quality of the script that you send is incredibly important, whether it is as an example of your writing or a radio
play that you hope will be commissioned. The first ten pages
are absolutely crucial. The radio producer or the reader at
BBC Writersroom may only get that far. Hopefully they will
love it and want to read on, but questions you should ask
yourself is: is it as good as it can possibly be? Could it do
with another edit? Have you read it out loud? What makes
this play good for radio? What excites you about it and what
slot do you think it is for?

And make sure the script looks professional. I know it seems
obvious but it's worth saying that, if your script looks tatty, it
will give the wrong impression from the start, and you are
trying to get into an overcrowded and incredibly competitive world. Character names should be on the left, sound
effects clearly marked and pages numbered. Have a look at
the example in Part Four of this book. Don't listen to writers
who say 'Well, I sent in my script in Final Draft and it was
fine.' Those days have gone. Presentation is important

because it makes reading quick and easy, and in a world where budgets are tight and time is precious, professionalism counts. There are more examples of script layout on the BBC Writersroom website but the universally preferred format is the one in this book. You will need to set up your own template as, at the time of writing, there isn't one available online.

Alongside your sample script it is important to develop several radio ideas that you would like to write in the future. This gives you the maximum chance of having something that you and the producer you are hoping to meet will be able to develop together. The producer may tell you that some of these ideas have been done very recently, or an idea might not be what the network is looking for at that moment. For example, there may be a moratorium on thrillers in the Afternoon Drama slot, or the commissioning editor may be actively discouraging medical stories because they are being heavily commissioned elsewhere. Subjects often crop up in clusters so, while being passionate about your ideas, be prepared to let them go. They might come back later as stage plays or television proposals.

4

Producers:
What They Do and What to Expect

Producers don't have commissioning power. Their job is to know what the BBC networks are looking for and offer new ideas to the commissioning editors once or twice during the year.

At a first meeting a producer will want to discuss the script that you have sent in. They will want to know if it is an example of the quality of your work or if it is a radio play that you would like to have commissioned. The producer obviously likes it or you wouldn't be there, but there may be various obstacles preventing it from getting commissioned. Its subject, or something very like it, may have been done recently, or the slot that it is most suited for is not open for bids at the moment. In which case the producer will move on to strategies to deal with this, and to discuss the other ideas that you have brought with you.

What should a new idea consist of at this stage? A title, if you know it. A few characters, particularly the central character. The gist of the story and the starting point, again if you know it, but you may not and that's fine. Most importantly, what is it that makes you want to write it? What is it about this idea that is so insistent that it *has* to be written? What makes you uniquely qualified to write it?

The producer wants to get a sense of the world that the play is set in and the feel of the play, for example 'a dark fable set in Afghanistan'. They may also have questions about the story and the characters which could be helpful when you come to develop them in more detail later. For example, because radio drama isn't great at giving the bigger picture, a producer might ask from whose point of view this story is being told.

> I produced a dramatisation of Sebastian Faulks's novel *Birdsong* for radio. He asked me how we were proposing to portray the Battle of the Somme. Battles of any kind can sound like six actors shouting in a cupboard, which is more or less how they are created. The listener doesn't know who they are following, what's happening or why they should care about it. In this case, the dramatist, Nick Stafford, put us in a shell-hole with one man. We follow the battle from the point of view of the central character, Stephen Wraysford. It was terrifying and very effective.

A producer is there to help, and they will be steering an idea towards a particular slot. If you are a first-time writer this is most likely to be the Afternoon Drama. The commissioning process is fiercely competitive so the producer will be looking for selling points for the idea as well as for you, the writer. For example, you may have thought of a high-profile actor that you would love to cast in your play. This could be a selling point. It doesn't guarantee that you will get that actor but it gives a producer and, at a later stage, the commissioning editor a picture of how you see the character.

> In first-time writer Christopher Harris's *Walk Right By Me*, the central character was a stalker. He followed a woman on the street, on the bus, in the park. He watched her in the pub and he followed her home. He even got into her house and went through her things when she wasn't there. His lonely obsession

and ordinariness to the point of invisibility was scary. I asked Chris who he thought ideally should play the part and he said Gary Oldman. So I sent Gary Oldman the script and within six weeks I heard that he was interested. The play was commissioned by Radio 4 on condition that Gary Oldman played the lead. Months of shenanigans followed before we finally agreed recording dates, but Chris got his first commission out of it and the play had a hugely appreciative response from listeners.

Another writer, Justin Butcher, had written a one-man show, *The Seven White Masks of Scaramouche Jones*, as a performance vehicle for himself. Scaramouche Jones was an observer on the sidelines of the great events of the twentieth century; a sort of Rosencrantz and Guildenstern in the body of a one-hundred-year-old clown. The play was his life story and how he acquired the seven white masks of the title. It was brilliant, touching, witty and fresh. It is unusual for monologues to be commissioned from first-time writers. In fact, monologues are rarely done at all because the writing has to be absolutely outstanding to keep the audience listening. It was Justin's idea to approach Warren Mitchell with the script. He loved it and the play was commissioned by Radio 4 with him on board. Both Warren Mitchell and Justin Butcher did a brilliant job. Pete Postlethwaite later won awards in a theatre version of the play and Justin has gone on to write many more plays for radio since.

There may be one or two practical considerations that come up in conversation with a producer. For example, if your idea hinges on a particular anniversary or birthday, then the date and any other crucial facts associated with it may need checking. If the play is a biography then a producer will probably ask what your source of information is. If it is in the public domain – that is to say, it is readily available in newspapers, books, on television and radio – then you are free to use it as you see fit; but if you want to use facts or quotes from a single source, such as a published biography, then the producer has to check that the rights are available. This ensures that the biographer is happy to have their work used and they get a small payment. You don't need to worry about this as it is the producer's job to sort this out; but it is important for writers to be accurate and honest about source material from the outset so there are no nasty surprises later.

If a play is about a living person or people, then there may be legal considerations. Do you need to get the subject's permission to use their story? Is their story in the public domain? Are any of the crucial events taken from a single source? Even if the central character is dead there will probably be family who need contacting. They certainly need to know that the play is being written. It is part of the BBC's remit that anyone portrayed in a drama or their close relatives will be informed and their backing sought for the project. This isn't the same as editorial control. No one has copyright on their life story if the information is in the public domain, but it obviously makes good sense to get the subject's cooperation from the start to avoid any misunderstandings. Again, it is the producer's job to make the necessary checks and they will be working from the information that the writer gives them. Don't be put off by this. It won't make your project any less attractive. In fact, it may make it more so. Producers like a challenge.

And finally a producer will want to know if you are talking to other radio producers – or theatres, or television – about any of these projects. It doesn't matter if you are. It could be a selling point. But it's important your producer knows so they don't waste time developing the same idea as someone else.

5

Frequently Asked Questions
from First-time Writers

1. What sort of language is allowable in an Afternoon Drama?

You're unlikely to find 'fuck', 'cunt' or 'nigger' here, although it's not impossible. Really strong language has to be agreed with the network controller. Some listeners don't like it, and some are deeply offended by it and switch off immediately; so there has to be a good argument for it. On television this kind of language is saved for after the nine o'clock watershed. On radio, strong language is rarely broadcast at all because the word is much more exposed. A radio play cannot contextualise the spoken word in the way that television does with, for instance, a reaction shot. The mental pictures the listener is creating are largely based upon the text. But language and our perception of it is changing all the time. If your radio play is going to be convincing then it's important that the dialogue reflects the world it is set in as authentically as possible and, like it or not, people do swear.

Contrary to popular belief there is no list of banned words on BBC radio. Is 'bollocks' acceptable at 2.30 in the afternoon? What about 'wanker' or 'piss off'? I think it all depends on the context and how often it is repeated. There is an argument for using 'creative swearing'. In Nick Warburton's comedy series *On Mardle Fen*, the central character, an eccentric celebrity chef reminiscent of Keith Floyd, uses the words 'underpants' and 'arse' as expletives and calls his son 'a complete pilchard'. Cornish writer Carl Grose used the same approach in his play *The Kneebone Cadillac*.

Where he might have used the word 'wanker' he used 'spanner'. It worked equally well.

2. What about sex in radio drama?

The Afternoon Drama has tackled everything from gay sex to straight sex, marital infidelity, rape, incest and paedophilia. There is no subject outside the scope of this slot. It all depends on how it is handled. What's the heart of the story? What's the point of telling it? Is it being told by the right person?

Portraying sex itself on radio can be tricky. As in real life it can sound embarrassing and ludicrous. The important thing to ask is what story are you telling at this point? How does the sex move the story on and in what way? What happens before the actual sex? What happens afterwards? Could these moments be more dramatically interesting than the sex itself?

3. What about violence in radio drama?

I think it all depends on how violence is handled, and a writer needs to ask broadly the same questions about it as they do about the portrayal of sex. What is the crux of the story you are telling? What happens before the violence? What happens after it and how much actual violence do we need to hear?

I produced a play called *I Am Emma Humphreys* by Shelley Silas, based on the true story of a homeless teenager. The real-life Emma Humphreys met a man on the streets of Nottingham, fell into a violent relationship with him and killed him in self-defence. She was convicted of murder but the conviction was eventually changed to manslaughter in a groundbreaking case.

> Emma's story was disturbing and violent, but she was a funny, creative and thoughtful person. Her upbeat character in the play contrasted with the bleak story that she was telling. It gave the listeners a way in. They cared about her even though she was not always likeable. The violence which she was subjected to was an integral part of her story. If Emma's successful appeal was based on self-defence then we had to show what she was defending herself from. Each attack was carefully thought about by the writer. Each one upped the stakes and added to the story. It wasn't a comfortable listen but it was a play that I am very proud of, and it won an award for portrayal of social issues.

4. Where will the play be recorded?

Radio plays don't have to be recorded in drama studios. It depends where your drama is set or if there a particular sound associated with it. Plays can be recorded on location. This often isn't as grand as it sounds. It may be a small flat on a housing estate, a school or a country house – in fact, anywhere that has the range of acoustics that your play needs. For example, I recorded Stephen Wyatt's *Party Animal* in my house and garden. It was set in the present and we used scrunchy gravel with a city background for the exteriors, and my bedroom, kitchen and living room for the interiors. The advantage of recording on location is that everything is real: real background noise, real furniture, real doors, real stairs and cellars. You get a great sound and actors love it. It can make their performances more realistic and you are in a space where they are more likely to bond as a company, which is also good for the play. Recording on location could be a selling point. The downside is you can spend a lot of time hanging about waiting for planes to pass overhead or for rain to stop, and you sometimes get interrupted by passers-by who see the microphone and dive in with things like 'Is this the Daz doorstep challenge?' I have recorded in cellars, underground bunkers, schools, theatres, on a canal boat, in a van, in woods and fields, on a roof and down a tin mine. It is slower than recording in a studio but the realistic sound and stellar performances you get make it a very tempting option when it is practical.

5. Can I have music in my play?

If specially composed music is an essential component then it is important to talk to the producer about it from the out-set. Original music is a luxury in radio drama. It adds considerably to the cost of the production so savings have to be made elsewhere, e.g. fewer actors. But it is not impos-sible, so don't rule it out entirely.

If you want to put titles and tracks of recorded music in your script then do. But don't feel you *have* to come up with the music. You can simply write 'music' in your script and the producer will find something suitable at the production stage. It is also the producer's job to check that the rights for the music are cleared for broadcast. The BBC, or the inde-pendent production company, then logs the duration of each track that is actually used and they pay a small sum to the musicians through the Performing Rights Society. This doesn't add significantly to the cost of the production so you don't need to worry about it.

*

By the end of your conversation with a producer, either a script or one or two ideas will have been selected for devel-opment. So what happens next?

6

Proposals and Offers

A writer will come away from a meeting with a producer having been asked to do one of a number of things. If you are developing an idea then you probably will have been asked to write it up in a bit more detail. This is about thinking it through rather than writing at length. Be succinct. A proposal only needs to be two or three paragraphs. One side of A4 is enough. You need the gist of the story and a title. Think about how the story starts. Who are we with? What is the world of the play? What is the tone and the genre? It is also useful to include a very brief summary of what else you've written, or any writers' group that you are part of. If there is anything else that you have written that relates to the idea that you are selling then add that too. It could be a stage play that has had a reading and is similar in style, or an article you've written which is about the same subject as your play. Mentioning this sort of thing can add substance to your idea and give it an air of confidence.

Meanwhile the producer is checking that the idea has not been done already and that no one else is currently pursuing the same subject in the same way. They are also carrying out any legal or factual checks.

When the Radio 4 commissioning process, or offers round, begins, all drama producers are invited to submit brief outlines of writers' ideas to the BBC. These are known as pre-offers and are designed to prevent large numbers of unwanted ideas from being developed. In the case of drama, a pre-offer consists of a synopsis of up to one hundred words. The Radio 4 guidelines give the following example:

'Brilliant seventeenth-century Danish Prince seeks to revenge the mysterious death of his father and in so doing loses his mind, destroys his family and overturns the state of Denmark. Renaissance tragedy. Period verse drama.' Yes, it's *Hamlet* – in thirty-five words. They also ask for an additional paragraph of up to 200 words saying why the writer wants to do the play, how they want to do it and why it would work on Radio 4. These are the selling points that the producer has gleaned from their conversation with you and from your written proposal.

The producer writes the pre-offer from the information you have given them. Here is an example of an actual pre-offer that I wrote using the information from the writer's proposal.

SE8 by Janice Okoh – a forty-five-minute Afternoon Drama

A seventeen-year-old girl is accidentally shot and killed in a London nightclub as a result of gang violence. Rita is positive that the police will find her daughter's murderer but they meet a wall of silence. Donna, seventeen, was there. She knows the gang who did it. She went to school with them. Detectives on the case are getting nowhere. Rita takes the law into her own hands and urges Donna to come forward. The police offer witness anonymity in court but it's not one hundred per cent guaranteed. Will Donna speak out? Will she survive if she does?

This play is about gang culture and about trying to get justice in a climate of fear. Opening with the shooting, the story is told from three points of view: the mother, the witness and the perpetrators. It is about bullying and being bullied, individual courage and the legal framework that protects it. Janice Okoh will interview ex-gang members in South London. She has access to an experienced policeman who deals with youth crime in the area so she is confident about her research. This play was inspired by the deaths of two Birmingham teenagers in 2003 and a Polish care-worker in 2007. Anonymous witnesses were used to help secure both convictions. In June 2008 the House of Lords overturned this practice. The Home Secretary reversed this decision a month later but a judge can still direct a jury to discount anonymous witness statements. Janice Okoh is an exciting black British voice. For R4: *A Short Ride to Düsseldorf* (British woman marries Nigerian for money) and *From Lagos with Love* (lawyer uncovers Nigerian oil fraud and falls for his contact). She is part of the Royal Court's Critical Mass Playwriting Group and has an MA in Screenwriting from the University of East Anglia.

What do you think made this pre-offer successful? Why does the writer want to tell this story? What are the selling points?

For scripted comedy the pre-offer is a maximum of 200 words in length and the synopsis and selling points are rolled into one. Here is an example of a comedy pre-offer which I wrote using information from the writer's proposal. It was commissioned as a series for late-night Radio 4.

Ida Barr – *Artificial Hip Hop* by Christopher Green
4 x fifteen-minute series

Ida is an eccentric music-hall singer who has embraced hip hop and rap. 'Missy Elliott meets Marie Lloyd' *Guardian*. She reflects the cultural diversity of London's East End where she has been living in retirement for several decades. Ida has a genuine love of talking to people so each week she investigates a topic (e.g. bingo, euthanasia, bendy buses) and engages with real people in real situations. Ida visits a Caribbean pensioners club, an after-school group of eight- to ten-year-olds or a workshop for Hackney's aspiring DJs. Character comedy meets documentary, with music.

Ida Barr is the creation of award-winning comedy performer and writer, Christopher Green. Stage shows include *Get Old Or Die Tryin'* and *Ida Barr's So This is Christmas* will be at the Barbican Theatre this December. Chris really flies when he is improvising and audiences love Ida's bizarre mix of sharp observation, music hall, rap and hip hop. The music and actuality will be linked by Ida's private thoughts recorded on her Ida-pod – an ancient battery-operated cassette machine with a greasy earpiece. Ida Barr is marvellously theatrical but everything around her is utterly real.

The Radio 4 commissioning team sifts the pre-offers over a two- or three-week period and shortlists the ones they think are most worth developing. If an idea is successful, writers get feedback via the producer. The commissioners don't provide feedback on the ones that are rejected. Any questions from Radio 4 arising from the pre-offer, or additional information they ask for, has to be quickly assembled by writer and producer during the brief period between the pre-offer results and the final offers deadline. The final offer is a maximum of two pages long (an expanded version of the pre-offer) and is written by the producer.

Here is an example of a full offer I wrote for a play by a first-time writer. The feedback we got from the pre-offer was to develop the narrative in as much detail as possible. Writer Matthew Hurt worked up a very full synopsis. We were also trying to show why this play would be of interest to the Radio 4 audience and why Matthew was uniquely qualified to write it.

Phumzile (pron: poom-zil-ee) by Matthew Hurt – a forty-five-minute Afternoon Drama

Summary

Set in South Africa and London exploring the complicated relationships we have with the developing world. Should we give through charities? Does charity foster dependency? How do we deal with approaches from individuals? Big themes housed in an intimate setting. An ambitious idea from a highly talented first-time writer to radio Matthew Hurt.

Synopsis

Tom, a black British man, and Pete, also British but white, are on holiday in South Africa. When a mugger tries to snatch Pete's mobile from him, a local woman, Phumzile, comes to Pete's assistance. As a way of thanking her, Pete invites her out for dinner. Tom predicts social catastrophe: she will be a fish out of water in Durban's swanky eateries. But after some initial awkwardness the evening is a success. Phumzile, in turn, insists that they visit her home in the nearby township. Pete accepts the invitation; Tom refuses, saying that two foreign tourists in a sparkling new hire car will be prime targets for attack. In Phumzile's house, furnished only with two chairs, a television, and a framed photo of an infant girl, she reveals she is HIV positive, has lost her youngest daughter to the disease (having passed it on in pregnancy) and has a strained relationship with her surviving daughter. Pete is sympathetic. This is the first time, she says, she has cried in front of a man. As it is now dark, Phumzile insists on accompanying Pete in his car until he is out of the township. Saying goodbye, Pete insists that she take some money from him. She accepts.

Less than a week after Tom and Pete's return to the UK, Phumzile calls. She can't afford next month's medication. Pete sends cash despite Tom's warning that he's being conned. As Phumzile's requests become more inflated, Tom is increasingly suspicious. But Pete refuses to be anything but trusting and pays for her to come over to London for further medical treatment. With all three of them living under one roof, the pressure mounts. Especially as Phumzile barely leaves her room and doesn't pull her weight in the household. Tom finally convinces Pete that Phumzile is exploiting them and the two men confront her. She says very little in her defence. Proof, Tom concludes, that he was right all along. Phumzile is instructed to pack her bags so that she can leave on the next flight. She insists that she isn't well enough to travel but this falls on deaf ears.

It's not until they get a call from the airline that they realise Phumzile is seriously ill. She hasn't been allowed to board the plane as she was coughing up blood in the departure lounge. Panicked, they rush Phumzile to hospital but she dies a week later. When the attendant doctor asks the men if she was on antiretroviral medication they report that she was. Judging by the speed with which pneumonia ravaged her body and killed her, the doctor is incredulous. Motivated partly by guilt, partly by a need to atone,

Tom and Pete arrange for Phumzile's body to be cremated and take the ashes back to South Africa. There they meet Phumzile's daughter and the mystery of Phumzile's apparent lethargy as well as her sudden death is explained. She'd not been taking her medication, but sending it back home for her daughter to sell on the black market as a source of income. By having her body cremated Pete has deeply offended her family. He is more of an outsider than ever and all he wanted to do was help.

Why this Afternoon Drama?

Matthew Hurt is an outstanding writer, new to radio, who explores large important themes through a small cast, housed in a convincing world that the R4 audience can relate to. This stunning new drama is about the complicated relationships we have with the developing world: our sense of guilt and our fear of being patronising. Should we give through charities? Does charity foster dependency? How do we deal with approaches from individuals? What should our personal response be to the suffering of others? Set partly in South Africa the themes of this play have a wider significance. The relationships are contemporary, touching and truthful. The characters are sharply observed. The tone is intimate, confessional and surprisingly humorous given the subject matter. The sound is naturalistic. An ambitious idea from a highly talented new writer.

In the drama we want to think the best of Phumzile but there is mounting evidence that she is conning Pete. As the tension between the three characters builds to a pitch, we are not sure who to believe. This is about rich and poor rather than black and white, and in the end both men are right. Phumzile is a con artist who puts her life on the line for very good reasons; so that her daughter can survive. A flawed heroine with flawed benefactors. The story reaches its dramatic climax in London. The last section in South Africa is a satisfying bookend to the drama. It is also refreshing to have two gay men who are not the centre of a drama involving HIV.

Matthew Hurt is South African so he knows what he is writing about. His aunt works in the largest public hospital in Durban. She has provided the HIV research for this play. Lethargy is a common symptom of HIV, which can kill the patient very quickly, particularly if they are not taking anti-retrovirals. The selling of these drugs to increase family income is an increasingly common problem in South Africa.

Matthew's writing includes *Believe* with Linda Marlowe at the Traverse Theatre and *Singing, Dancing, Acting* with Simon Callow at Soho Theatre. He won the Peggy Ramsay bursary to develop a stage play, *The Time Step*, and he has just been awarded Arts Council funding to open it at the Traverse Theatre. *Greed, Lust, Envy*, three linked monologues by Matthew Hurt, are attached to this offer to show the quality of his writing. His full writing CV is also attached.

Radio 3 commissions a much smaller amount of drama than Radio 4 and in consequence has a slightly simpler system. The commissioning editor doesn't require pre-offers. He or she only asks for a full offer which is more or less the same in content and length as that for Radio 4, i.e. two sides of A4 containing a brief summary of the proposal, a synopsis and compelling reasons why this drama should be commissioned. As with Radio 4, this offer is written by the producer from the information given to them by the writer.

In Conclusion

There is no denying that the offers process is a stressful and time-consuming business for both writers and producers, but that is the system and it is a great deal faster than in television. The results are sent out to all BBC and independent producers about two months after the offers round closes. In the case of Radio 4, this is usually in July or early August. Radio 3 results get sent to producers in October or November.

Getting the results is a heart-stopping moment. There has been a lot of investment from both of you. Writers get brief feedback from the commissioning editors on all offers, even the unsuccessful ones, through their producers. But the results are final. The writer is either offered a commission, the idea is rejected or, in a very few cases, it is shortlisted, which means there are still one or two things to clarify before a final decision is made.

What to Do if Things Go Wrong

What should you do if your proposal doesn't get a commission? First talk to your producer about why it wasn't successful. Don't forget this is an incredibly competitive market. Many other ideas didn't get in at all or didn't get beyond the pre-offers stage, so you should take some heart from that. But don't revamp and submit something that has been rejected. If the idea didn't succeed the first time then let it go. Set yourself a deadline to think of something new and a rough date when you think you will be ready to talk to your producer about it. If the new idea is not to their taste they can point you towards someone else who will like it. Go back to your radio-drama diary. Is there a producer there who you thought of contacting the first time around and didn't? If you have several new ideas it may be worth contacting more than one producer. Drama is subjective and what appeals to one producer may not appeal to another, and you are building useful working relationships with people who want to help you succeed. Don't despair. The rejected proposal may come round at another time as a stage play, a film, a short story or the basis of a novel, so don't throw it away.

Postscript

And Matthew Hurt got his commission for *Phumzile* by the way!

PART FOUR

Production

CLAIRE

1

The Commission: Getting Ready to Write

So what happens once you have got a commission? The first thing is you get sent a contract. This is a formal agreement between you and the BBC, or independent production company, to deliver the script. The production will have been roughly scheduled by BBC Radio for the following year, e.g. 'third quarter 2013'. This is when it is due to be 'on air'. Your producer will discuss with you dates for first and final drafts and for recording. If, for example, you are offered a commission for an Afternoon Drama in July 2013, the delivery schedule you agree, depending on your other commitments, might look something like this:

- First draft November 2013

- Final draft May 2014

- Record and edit June 2014

- Broadcast July 2014

All this information goes in the contract.

Deadlines are both frightening and energising, but they are there to be met. If for any reason you are going to be late delivering, tell your producer immediately. Life is complicated. Disasters happen. They know that. Producers are on your side and they will do their best to help you.

A first-time writer for radio, with no other writing track record, will currently be offered, at the time of writing, approximately £62 per minute for two broadcasts, which means that the BBC can repeat it within two years with no additional payment. The rate for experienced writers creeps up by small amounts with each play. These rates are negotiated annually with the BBC by the Writer's Guild and the Society of Authors. Their websites will have the most up-to-date information and their addresses are in the Resources section of this book.

Make sure that whoever is issuing your contract, i.e. BBC Copyright or the independent company producing your work, knows what your writing experience is. Send them a CV. Your track record in non-drama writing could also lift you off the bottom rung, so don't forget to show it. You don't need an agent at this point. If the person issuing the contract has your writing CV then the fee you are offered will be broadly correct. If you are unsure then it is worth checking how the fee was arrived at. If you have an agent they will do this for you, so make sure they have your up-to-date CV, including any relevant non-drama writing. The fee for a radio play is not large but no one wants to cheat you. The writer is what this project is all about at this point.

Before you get down to writing the first draft, there are one or two things that you can do that could be helpful later. You could ask to sit in on a drama recording. If you are working with a BBC producer this is easy to arrange: there are dramas being recorded all year round. Watching actors and a director working on someone else's play could be incredibly useful, and you'll get to meet another writer. Independent companies produce a smaller volume of work but an independent producer should still be able to arrange for you to observe a recording.

Check the cast size so you are writing for the right number of actors. Radio budgets are small and usually agreed at the beginning of the project. If you want to bring in an extra character, ask yourself: do you really need them? Is there another way round it? If you want the actors to double then be realistic. If there are only three actors in your play, you might get away with one of them delivering the odd line as a station announcer or distant waiter, but any more than that and the audience will notice. And some actors are too recognisable to double, so you are restricting casting options at a very early stage. Offering to play minor parts yourself doesn't solve the problem: strictly speaking, you still have to be paid.

Are there any crucial facts to check? If you are working on a biographical play and using information from a single source then check with your producer that the rights are available. If you are writing about real people in the present or recent past, make sure, by asking your producer, that they, or their relatives, know that your drama is going ahead. Hopefully they will have given the project their blessing and you may even want to meet them for research purposes.

Don't worry at this stage about naming products and commercial organisations, e.g. Hoover, Tesco, Microsoft, etc., as long as you are not deliberately advertising. Branding is very much part of our culture and radio drama reflects this, especially in comedy. Even if a character says something unflattering about a product it can be perfectly acceptable depending on who is saying it, how often and in what context. If you're not sure, ask your producer. It is their job to follow the BBC guidelines on this and advise you accordingly. The producer is there to help. No question is too small.

2

What Should Your Script Look Like?

It is important that your script looks tidy and professional at all stages. Every script should have a title page with a contact address in the bottom left-hand corner. Always include a phone number and an email address. If you have an agent, their address and phone number can go here too, and put a draft number and a date on the title page. A cast list on a separate page is also useful but you don't need to include a synopsis and you don't need to put title, writer's name and contact details on every page.

When actors are recording radio drama they read from the script, so having the characters' names on the left and clear of the dialogue is important for visual clarity. Sound engineers want to pick out backgrounds and sound effects quickly, so it helps to put them in capitals, clear of dialogue, and underlined. And keeping all stage directions to a minimum also helps reduce the number of pages that actors are holding in their hands as they record.

Here is a sample script layout from the BBC Radio Drama Department. At the time of writing this is the preferred industry format. You will see variations on the BBC Writersroom website but this is the one to go for. BBC producers have started sending the template out to writers on commission, particularly to first-time writers. At the moment, this template is not available from any other source, but it is fairly simple to set it up yourself using the instructions contained in this sample scene.

WHAT SHOULD YOUR SCRIPT LOOK LIKE?

EPISODE 1

SCENE 1	**INT: THE OFFICE**
FX:	COGS WHIRRING IN B/G – SOUND EFFECTS
	SHOULD BE IN CAPS AND UNDERLINED

CHARACTER: The dialogue goes here and set the hanging ident at 4.5cms.

ANOTHER: The font is Arial and the size is 13. Line spacing is 1.5. It should look very clear.

CHARACTER: Number the pages and, if it's a series, include the Episode Number at the top or bottom of the page.

ANOTHER: Double check that the hanging indent is set at 4.5 cms for the text and that you have set the first tab at 1.25cms for the CHARACTER NAME.

CHARACTER: (STAGE DIRECTIONS TO ACTORS SHOULD BE IN CAPS AND BRACKETED) Setting out a script in this way makes it easier for the actors to read.

ANOTHER: There's no need for you to number the speeches. They will change during different drafts. The Broadcast Assistant, known at the BBC as a Production Coordinator, will add speech numbers to the final draft.

1

EPISODE 1

CHARACTER: Don't worry about splitting speeches over the page or writing 'continued' next to a speech that goes over two pages. The Production Coordinator will decide which page the speech will go on and mark it accordingly at final draft stage

ANOTHER: (V.O.) *Voiceover indicates a character who is narrating over sound, music or dialogue. Always type narration or voice-overs in italics or bold.*

EPISODE 1

<u>SCENE 2</u>   **<u>EXT: THE PARK</u>**

Each scene starts on a separate page, so put in a page break after each one.

Here is an extract from the BBC Writersroom website with a number of common terms you can use for telescoping dialogue:

CHARACTER 1:   (OFF) Indicates that the actor should speak at a distance from the microphone. The audio equivalent of 'off-screen'.

CHARACTER 2:   (CLOSE) Indicates that the actor should be in close proximity to the microphone, giving an intimate feel to the dialogue.

CHARACTER 1:   (LOW) Indicates that the actor should speak quietly, almost in a whisper – or you can simply write 'whispers'.

CHARACTER 2:   (DISTORT) Indicates a character who is speaking via a mechanical device such as a telephone or radio.

*

On the subject of stage directions, the golden rule is 'less is more'. If, for example, you have a scene set in a busy supermarket and the characters are by the tills, then say so. You don't need to add that there is chat from shoppers, crying babies, food being packed in plastic bags, etc. The same applies to stage directions for actors. Actors don't need 'heatedly', 'nervously' or 'angrily' preceding their lines. What's needed should be clear in the writing. The instruction 'laughs heartily' is guaranteed to produce an unconvincing squawk. Only use stage directions if you are asking actors to convey something that is not clear in the dialogue and action, for example, if a line is ironic rather than literal.

How long should your script be? As Stephen has already written, the script for a forty-five-minute Afternoon Drama is roughly 8,000 words, including stage directions. If there are lengthy monologues or a great deal of narration the word count should be lower because narration plays slower than fast, overlapping dialogue. To really check the length of a first draft there is no substitute for reading it out loud. This is also a chance to give it a further edit and get rid of lurking typos.

If your first draft for an Afternoon Drama is much too long, i.e. over 10,000 words, don't send it. The play will probably not only need cutting; it will need restructuring. A writer once sent me the first draft of an Afternoon Drama weighing in at a hefty 20,000 words. I rang him before reading it and urged him to make cuts unless he was 'really in trouble'. He said he was: he couldn't see the wood for the trees. So I began reading with a heavy heart, knowing that more than half of the play would have to be thrown away. I realised it was more productive to mark what I thought we should keep than mark what should be cut. Each scene had to earn its place, starting later and ending earlier. The audience often don't need as much steering as we think they do. The play emerged slimmer and fitter and the writer gave it a new radio-friendly ending: one of the characters confiding to the audience, a device which enabled the writer to link tiny dramatic highpoints salvaged from discarded scenes. But unless you are totally lost it is better to shape and shave a first draft yourself without interference from a producer.

3

You've Delivered Your First Draft:
What Happens Next?

The producer will contact you to arrange a meeting to discuss it. Letting someone read your script for the first time
can be nerve-racking, but there are ways you can prepare for
this. Having set aside the play for a week or two, re-read it
and decide for yourself what is working and what is not.
Write down these 'notes to self' and take them to the meeting. I produced Charlotte Jones's first original play for radio,
Mary Something Takes the Veil, about a novice nun who
takes a vow of silence – a bit of a challenge on radio! I began
the meeting by asking her how she would like to see the play
develop; what did she think were its strengths and weaknesses? Without a moment's hesitation Charlotte rattled off
five succinct points. I glanced down at my notes and there
were the same five points, and nothing else. We were obviously going to get along – and the meeting was going to be
very short. Charlotte went on to win the Critics' Circle and
Susan Smith Blackburn Awards for her stage play *Humble
Boy*. I directed her witty dramatisation of Roald Dahl's
Matilda and she is currently adapting *Pride and Prejudice*
for Radio 4's Classic Serial, as well as writing for television.
Charlotte was always a sharp critic of her own work, but I
think this is a skill that most writers can learn.

Script Meetings: Some Thoughts from Stephen

In television, particularly when working on a drama series, you can receive notes which have everything to do with the internal politics of the production department or the latest bee in the bonnet of the executive producer, and very little to do with your script. When I worked on television series, I often used to come out of script meetings with my brain scrambled and my confidence at rock bottom. But in radio this just isn't the case. The main thing to remember is that your producer is giving you notes because he/she wants to help you to create a really good radio drama. There is no other agenda.

So try and be relaxed and not too defensive about what the producer tells you. Of course, some producers are better than others at pinpointing what's not working in your script, but everything they tell you, however misguided it may seem at the time, you must consider carefully. Because, even if their suggestions about how to fix what's wrong don't chime with yours, they are telling you that something isn't quite working and it needs to be fixed. A novelist friend of mine calls it 'raising a red flag'.

But, more often, your producer's suggestions are perceptive and helpful and you'd be crazy not to incorporate them into your rewrites – because they're going to make your play work better. This doesn't mean that you agree blindly to every suggestion and end up going home with a list of changes you don't really want to make. If you have a good reason for what you've written and the producer hasn't grasped it, you should say so. If you've done something which is clumsy and doesn't do the business, then acknowledge that too. A script meeting is part

> of a creative collaboration and the building of mutual
> trust and respect.
>
> So stay calm and listen. You really do have nothing
> to lose.

Another useful tip is to take a hard copy of your script with you to the meeting. A producer's notes are usually a mixture of a general overview of the play and specific suggestions, so you need a script to refer to.

If the producer says something isn't working, find out what the problem is. The producer may offer solutions but you might think of something better. You are the world expert on your play, but the producer knows the network, the slot and the listeners. By working creatively together you can deliver what was promised in the offer, or something even better.

It is important to be clear about what the producer is asking you to do. Are you being asked to alter the emphasis on something or remove it altogether? To reshape a few scenes or rewrite the play from top to bottom? Take notes so you have something to refer to and think about afterwards. You will also be deciding together what are the strengths of this first draft: great moments, scenes and characters which can be built on. It's important not to throw out the baby with the bath water.

Common Problems

One of the most common first-draft problems is getting the story shape right. It is often too slow at the beginning, when you were feeling your way into writing it, and now it needs to get going more quickly to make space later for other things. So I might ask a writer: is this the right place to start your story? Can you get into the opening scenes quicker? Can you come out of them faster?

Sagging middles are another first-draft problem. You have created a terrific set-up. The story whips along in the first twenty pages and then the scenes and the characters seem to be marking time. So I might ask you if you need these scenes – are they earning their place by pushing the story on? Are you perhaps telling us too much? Bryony Lavery, writer of *Frozen* for the National Theatre and more recently *Beautiful Burnout* for the National Theatre of Scotland, says another good question to ask at this point is: has everyone met everyone in the play? This could generate a new scene which could give the sagging middle a lift.

Endings can be another problem. If they are too neat they lack credibility. If they are not neat enough they are unsatisfying. If you were telling this story to a group of friends, the ending would let them know why you were telling it in the first place. The basic mechanics of storytelling are imprinted in our DNA but it's easy to lose sight of them in the complex process of playwriting. The key to solving an endings problem usually lies much earlier in the play. Questions I might ask a writer are: what was the incident or event which kick-started your drama? What was at stake for the main characters? What did they want to know, test or discover? What was the result? By the end of the play, have they changed in any way? How do we know that? The questions are an attempt to open up possibilities. A satisfying ending is usually a mixture of logic and imagination with a small dash of the unexpected. There are no right or wrong answers.

Sometimes in a first draft the scenes don't contrast enough with each other. One scene merges into the next, making it all sound a bit flat and formless. One of the things I might ask a writer to look at is the balance of indoor and outdoor settings. I might ask if that office scene could be reset in a gym, or on a dance floor; in a tent or up a mountain. And if a character is speaking at the end of a scene and has the opening line in the next scene then producers usually ask the writer to give the opening line to another character so the scene junction is more clearly defined.

The play is probably too long at this point so what do you cut? The producer will have suggestions. We are experienced script editors, but it is your play. I look at how each scene connects to the central idea. Does each one progress the story? I look at the top and bottom of scenes. Can we get in and out more quickly? Can you say in one line what you are currently saying in three? The audience is sharp; they will fill in the gaps and enjoy doing it.

A final question that I might ask a writer is: what haven't you put in the play that you'd love to have put in? I have shamelessly stolen this question from Bryony Lavery. It encourages you to be bold and imaginative; decide what's missing and go for it, even if the idea seems a bit left-field. It might not work for you but try it and see.

A writer usually comes away from a first-draft meeting with a lot to do. You will have agreed a deadline for the next draft and be buzzing with ideas. Later, when you sit down to write, if something isn't clear, or you are weighing up a couple of possibilities and you are not sure which one to choose, then contact your producer. They are there to help.

Second Draft and Beyond

A similar process may occur at second draft. Writer and producer meet and go over the new draft together and agree any further changes. If the play is pretty much ready, this meeting may happen on the phone or by email. A third or final draft is often no more than a few small adjustments, to make sure it is the right length, and any typos are tidied up. Meanwhile the producer is doing any final factual or legal checks, or language referrals, and checking that any fictional names could not be mistaken for those of real people and that references to commercial products are not defamatory. When the final draft is finished the producer authorises the release of the rest of the writer's fee and moves on to preparing for recording.

If you have any casting suggestions for your play then do tell your producer, but don't worry if you don't have any. It is the producer's job to cast the play appropriately, bearing in mind the limitations of the budget.

We have some of the best actors in the world here in the UK and most of them want to work in radio drama because the scripts are good, there is a high level of directorial and technical expertise during the recording and the time commitment for actors is small. In the last year alone I have heard Bill Nighy, Judi Dench, Meera Syall, Patrick Stewart, Lenny Henry, Juliet Stevenson, Sarah Lancashire, Paterson Joseph and Benedict Cumberbatch all acting brilliantly in radio plays. Hosting the BBC Audio Drama Awards in 2013, actor David Tennant said:

> Acting on the radio is challenging, inspiring, delicate and always a privilege. Radio drama is often overlooked and undervalued next to its showier younger siblings on the television and in the cinema, and yet it is on the wireless that so many important and brilliant talents have been discovered and nurtured. The quality of our radio drama is one of the things that makes me proud to be British.

4

The Recording

A forty-five-minute Afternoon Drama will normally be recorded over two days. The BBC has recording studios in Edinburgh, Manchester, Birmingham, Belfast, Bristol, London and Cardiff and there are commercial studios used by independent drama producers in all of those places. Writers are invited to attend the recording and will be paid travel expenses if they live a substantial distance (fifty miles or more) from the studio or recording location, though lunch is not generally part of the deal.

The first day of recording usually starts with a readthrough and everyone gets given a recording schedule, if they haven't already been sent one. Scenes are often recorded in location rather than in story order. For example, in *On Mardle Fen* by Nick Warburton, the comedy drama series set in a restaurant in rural Cambridgeshire, we recorded all the riverbank scenes together. It is usually quicker to move actors rather than objects, so once the mics and the grass on the studio floor were in place and the background bird-calls had been found, we recorded everything for which this set-up was required. This gave us valuable extra time to spend on other things, such as fine-tuning performances and tricky scenes scrambling in and out of an attic.

The readthrough is both nerve-racking and exciting. This is the moment when the writer gets to meet the actors for the first time, and the only chance that you and the producer have to hear the whole play in the right order. The readthrough is timed. Only the dialogue is read, not the stage directions. Later, as each scene is recorded, the timing is measured against that of the readthrough, so at any point the producer can see if the play is going to be too long or too short. Timing is not an exact science. One actor's pacing may differ very much from another's and yet both can sound absolutely right.

Other people you will meet at the recording include the sound engineer (known as a studio manager at the BBC), who records and mixes the production. There may be a second sound engineer who in a drama studio provides pre-recorded sound, e.g. birdsong, car engines, pigs snuffling, or they might be on microphone with the actors, opening doors, chopping vegetables or climbing ladders. On a very complex production there are sometimes three sound engineers, but this is a luxury. You will also meet the broadcast assistant or production coordinator. Their role is to work with the producer coordinating all the practical aspects of the recording. They time each take, mark which are the best ones in preparation for editing, keep an eye on the schedule and note actors' arrival and leaving times. Writers are paid a fee for attending the recording. All writers get the same amount (currently £60 per day) and it is the production coordinator who makes sure they get it.

Just as it is the writer's responsibility to deliver the script in as complete a form as possible for the recording, it is the producer's responsibility to deliver the finished production on time, on budget and within BBC broadcast guidelines. It is the producer who is in charge of the production and coordinates the whole operation. During the recording, the writer's main function is to listen really carefully and pass any thoughts or notes via the producer when they are invited to do so. The producer will be busy positioning actors on microphone, checking background sound effects, making edit notes, etc., so the writer is the one person who can sit quietly and take in the whole effect of a scene. It is important not to jump in too early so that the production team and the actors have a chance to get things right. It is also important to *only give any comments through the producer* and to keep the comments as brief as possible.

Scenes are usually recorded in two or three takes so the production team and actors move quickly. The actors have scripts in their hands and if the scene asks for entrances and exits, cooking, fighting, bashing down doors or any other kind of action, the team are on the move and doing it – or rather what sounds like it. Umbrellas substitute for flapping bird wings, wet paper for vomit, metal hole-punchers for squeaky pram wheels and bananas for food of any kind because the mushy texture means actors can eat and speak at the same time. Coming up with the right-sounding props and live effects can be gloriously inventive and a joy to be part of.

The writer will be invited by the producer to give any comments at the end of a take, and they will check that the writer is happy before moving on to the next scene. The writer may also be asked to adjust a line if something isn't clear. Or if the play is too long or too short you will be asked for cuts or additional material. This can be a high-pressure moment. It is much better to cut on paper than leave it to chance in the edit, where an obvious cut may not be possible because an actor emphasises a line in a particular way or because the action will sound chopped. Cutting during the recording gives the writer more control. If the play is too short (and this rarely happens) it is useful to have brought copies of earlier drafts with you: there may be something in them that can be reinstated. Check with the producer exactly how much time you have to fill. As a useful ready reckoner, three words equals roughly one second.

I mentioned earlier the advantages of recording on location. The team and the writer's role in it are much the same as in a recording studio. The difference is the sound engineer and the producer will be moving with the actors and listening to them on headphones. For practical reasons you may only be able to hear the scenes live: three sets of headphones with trailing leads is an accident waiting to happen. But you will still get a good sense of how things are going and you can ask to listen on headphones at the end of a take. It is amazing how sensitive the microphones are: a passing car can sound like Concorde and a fridge motor can drown out actors in a kitchen.

Actors and sound engineers are incredibly good at what they do and the speed at which they work is truly astonishing, so it is good manners at the end of a recording for writers to give them a verbal thank you. There is no usual or formal way to mark the end of a recording. Sometimes everyone goes for a drink together but more often than not the studio empties. What happens is determined by the group of people who have been working on the production.

5
Post-production

Editing

The production is the producer's responsibility so, unless there has been a special agreement beforehand, the writer isn't usually present during editing. The sound engineer roughly assembles the play from the script marked up by the production coordinator. They then work with the producer substituting takes, adding music and sound effects, and generally polishing the production. A writer might be asked to listen to a playback or a rough-cut – there is still time for adjustments at this point – but this is a rarity. Stephen says he has never heard a preliminary playback of any of his radio dramas.

Editing occasionally involves radical decision-making, for example, savage cutting if the play is much too long. If this is the case the writer will be consulted. The Society of Authors recommends this and it is worth having a look at their website which has other useful pointers about the writer/producer relationship.

Restructuring a play in edit is rare, but it can happen and the writer should be consulted. With Mike Bartlett's first radio play, *Not Talking*, which I produced, we decided during edit to try swapping round the first two scenes. The play as originally written opened with a scene for an older couple in which they remember the past, from different perspectives. It was beautifully written but it wasn't typical of the gritty drama that was to come. It could have been the beginning of a Radio 4 Afternoon Drama, and *Not Talking* was going out in Radio 3's cutting-edge new writing slot, The Wire.

Below is the original opening. We discover in the course of the play that eighty-two-year-old James, played by Richard Briers, was a conscientious objector in World War Two who betrayed his wife Lucy, played by June Whitfield. Both characters talk directly to us.

From *Not Talking* by Mike Bartlett

FX:	PIANO MUSIC – CHOPIN'S NOCTURNES – CONFIDENTLY PLAYED BY LUCY.
JAMES:	I remember as a boy, I used to speak to everyone and anyone, incessantly. I found talking easy and I remember looking with curiosity at those other kind of people who were shy, or tongue-tied, and wonder what that must be like. To find speaking difficult.
	I'm James.
	I'm eighty-two.
	I live with my wife Lucy in a small cottage in Sussex.
	Very settled really.
LUCY:	I try not to remember the day when it happened. When we sat, stunned and still, his hand on mine, both of us crying. Not speaking.
JAMES:	I met Lucy just before the war at a friend's dinner party. She was nineteen. Beautiful.
LUCY:	But every morning at half past eight when I wake up I still scratch my stomach. I scratch. How uncouth. Scratch scratch. A distraction.

JAMES: Once married, we had a wonderful summer. Walking, punting, drinking, laughing.

LUCY: I will try to smile.

JAMES: One day, on a hill, I developed a glint in my eye, so I asked her what she thought of my idea. She smiled and said 'of course!' So we began to try after that.

LUCY: If you force yourself to smile when you're sad, you feel better.

(BEAT)

There. It actually works. Just think of the good times. Lemonade.

JAMES: Only three weeks later, she went for a test, and she was, so she came home and we celebrated with lemonade I think and going to bed and making love, but carefully because we didn't want anything to go wrong.

LUCY: Remember good times only. Drifting up the Thames on a punt. A summer's evening. Sunlight trembling through trees. Wireless playing. We lost the pole in the river and didn't care. Drifting with nothing to do.

JAMES: Did I listen to her womb to see if I could hear her inside? Yes.

FX: QUIET CRACKLING OLD RECORDING OF 'ME AND MY GIRL'.

JAMES: I sung to her. Could she hear me singing?

(HE SINGS OUT OF TIME TO THE MUSIC)

<u>FX:</u>	<u>THE RECORD SUDDENLY STOPS.</u>
LUCY:	We switched it off as we wanted to hear the birds and the water. And I'm sure people were being disturbed by the noise.
JAMES:	One day the midwife asked us if we would prefer a son or a daughter. And of course we replied that it didn't matter to us, but she continued that in her opinion, judging from the sudden aggressive kicks Lucy was feeling, it was probably a girl. Probably. So almost without thinking we named her Mary. Then two days later it happened.

In the second scene, Mark, played by Carl Prekopp, is a young soldier about to go to Iraq who meets fellow soldier Amanda, played by Lyndsey Marshal, at a party at the barracks. The young peoples' story, reminiscent of incidents at Deepcut and Catterick army barracks, frames the older couple's story throughout the play until Mike Bartlett cleverly weaves them together at the end.

In the edit we asked ourselves: should we open with the young soldier close-mic and full of bravado? It would have an immediate impact on the listeners. They would know something terrible was going to happen. We could follow it with the James/Lucy scene, but was this true to the spirit of the play? We consulted Mike and he joined us in edit to hear how swapping round the two scenes would sound. We decided it was a big improvement. So this is the opening that we actually used. It seems such an obvious solution now that I don't know why we didn't think of it earlier.

FX:	SHARP COCKING OF AN SA80 RIFLE.
MARK:	Crack crack crack. Or should I say t t t t t t t t t t t t t . Cos this is a standard SA80 Rifle with two settings… single-shot and semi-automatic.
	Beautiful weapon.
	(BEAT)
	Wicked.
	t t t t t t t t t t t t t t t
	At first we only got to use handguns… but, what it is, is that… with handguns you've got to be skilled. You have to aim. No. No point mate. Just shoot everywhere. See what you hit.
	(HE LAUGHS)
	For my seventeenth birthday, I remember my mum made me a sponge cake in the shape of a machine gun to celebrate me signing up. When Dad came round he said it was tasteless. He didn't even have a bit.
AMANDA:	I remember…
MARK:	But yeah… Amanda… yeah… She was a hottie.
AMANDA:	I remember he had this way with words.
MARK:	Sugar honey.
AMANDA:	When he swore, it sounded wrong, which was…
MARK:	Just sweet.

AMANDA: …Sweet.

MARK: All the lads thought she was. I did too.

AMANDA: He held his head at this funny angle. Which was…

MARK: They all wanted to do her.

AMANDA: What's the word… like… innocent?

MARK: She was well fit.

AMANDA: No. Endearing.

MARK: Nice tits Gary said.

AMANDA: Endearing.

(PAUSE)

Sensitive.

He just seemed different.

There was this like little party thing in the NAAFI and we all thought it would be crap cos drinks weren't allowed. But Kate brought the vodka and we got hammered. Me and the girls pissed up and dancing.

MARK: Her lot were new and the party was the Sergeant's idea to… um… bond as a unit. Gary said he'd like to bond with her as a unit.

I didn't really know what he meant.

Not Talking was broadcast in 2006 and repeated in 2007 in Radio 3's The Wire series. It was produced by Claire and directed by Steven Canny. It went on to win the Tinniswood Award for Best Radio Play and the Imison Award for Best

First Play on Radio in 2007, an exceptional double first; and Mike has been writing for radio ever since.

Publicity

Any writer wants as large an audience for their play as possible, so publicity is important. It is the producer's job to supply the relevant BBC publicity department with a press release containing information about the play, the writer and the cast. If the writer has specific interest or local press contacts then these should be put to good use too. The more press coverage the better, but it is important the writer liaises with the producer so the publicity department isn't covering the same ground.

A writer may be asked to do press interviews. This is pretty rare, although local papers may want to pick up the story. You are more likely to be asked to write a blog for the BBC Radio Drama website. Online insight into drama productions is much more common than it used to be and is very much encouraged by BBC and independent producers. BBC Writersroom may also be interested in hearing about your play and your experiences recording it, particularly if it has come through one of the schemes or competitions that they have promoted. If this is the case, talk to them.

Writers and producers commonly use Facebook, Twitter or their websites to tell friends when their drama is on. And you can make the broadcast an event. Annamaria Murphy's Afternoon Drama *Rosie's Beauty* was set in the Cornish village of Mousehole. When it was broadcast, local people gathered in the Methodist Hall to listen and share tea and cake. A whole school in Penzance listened to the play in their sports hall. You could hear *Ballad of the Burning Boy* by Lavinia Murray, written for Radio 3's The Wire, on a walking trail in Preston. Produced by Melanie Harris from Sparklab, the walking trail was part of their vision for the project from the start. Following the action on iPods around the city allowed listeners to experience the play differently. It gave the play a longer life and encouraged the participation of an audience who didn't necessarily listen to radio drama. New technology such as smartphone apps and podcasts are opening up all sorts of new possibilities for the way audiences receive radio drama, so if you have a idea about how this might work for your play, don't keep it to yourself.

6

Getting Your Second and Third Commission

Once your first play has been produced, the big hurdle is to get a second one commissioned. Getting your second or third commission can sometimes be harder than getting your first. Commissioning editors and producers want to encourage new writers. They want to encourage established writers too but there are a limited number of opportunities and a great many people bidding for them.

It is up to you to be proactive, to have new ideas by the time your play is broadcast and to contact your producer with them. If they don't like them they will pass you on to someone else who does. If your producer is too busy to take on your next idea or seems reluctant do so, ask them to recommend someone else. Or go back to your radio-drama diary and make contact with a producer whose work you've liked. As writers progress, it is quite usual for them to work with different producers and, by accident or design, they gradually build up a small network of people they like working with. Stephen has worked with me on various projects but also with other BBC producers, and he also works regularly with independents. He pitches ideas through both BBC and independent producers, judging what their different tastes are and who is most likely to get him his next commission. Successful producer/writer relationships can last for years. You build up a trust in each other and develop a shorthand which makes the creative process easy and joyful. The downside for the writer of working with one producer is that, if they cannot take on your next idea for any reason (illness, retirement, workload), you can feel suddenly cut adrift. Again, be proactive. Contact someone whose work you like. Producers are there to help you.

Any ideas you have for dramatisations are more likely to be considered once you have secured at least two commissions for original dramas. You will have developed a feel for radio as an art form in itself and be discovering how to use its imaginative possibilities. Talk to your producer about novels that you would like to dramatise and find out from them what the BBC networks have done recently and what they are looking for. Dramatisation ideas can also come from the producer but, as Stephen says in the section on dramatisations in this book, it is important that you genuinely like the novel you are being offered as you are going to be spending a lot of time with it.

Ideas for series are also more likely to be successful if you have had at least two single plays commissioned, but there is no hard-and-fast rule. Writers new to radio are regularly commissioned to write series for the 11 p.m. slot on Radio 4 but they must have a strong writing track record on the comedy circuit. If you have a great idea for a series, talk to your producer about it. It could start life as a single Afternoon Drama and develop into a series later. Your producer can help you find the best way forward for your idea. If they can't help they will point you in the direction of another producer who can.

When ideas get rejected it is invariably dispiriting but, as I have already mentioned, you can always turn a redundant radio idea into a stage play, or a television proposal. I heard writer and journalist Clare Bayley talking on Radio 4 about her play *Blue Sky*, which was about extraordinary rendition. I produced her first Afternoon Drama *The Secret Place*. *Blue Sky* was her second radio play and we tried very hard to persuade Radio 4 to commission it. We failed and two years later it was commissioned by Pentabus Theatre Company and later transferred to Hampstead Theatre. That's a determined writer for you.

PART FIVE

Notes on Comedy

CLAIRE

Comedy

Getting commissioned in radio comedy is broadly the same as in drama. You need a good idea, evidence of your writing ability and contact with a producer. A track record in live comedy also helps but it is not essential. There are BBC and independent producers who specialise in comedy, just as there are those who specialise in drama, but there is a fair amount of crossover between the two. A drama producer won't be in charge of a sketch or panel show but they will probably have produced some scripted comedy. I am principally a drama producer but I have also produced, amongst other things, four series of *Tina C* by Christopher Green, the satirical audio diary of a spoof country and western singer, and four dramatisations of Terry Pratchett's Discworld novels for the late-night comedy slot on Radio 4.

Unlike drama, BBC Radio Comedy has a direct relationship with television. Radio comedy is part of the BBC television comedy department, so television comedy classics like *Alan Partridge: Knowing Me, Knowing You* created by Steve Coogan, Armando Iannucci and Patrick Marber, *The League of Gentlemen* by Jeremy Dyson, Mark Gatiss, Steve Pemberton and Reece Shearsmith and *Little Britain* by David Walliams and Matt Lucas all started life as radio series. More recent examples of radio series being developed for television include *Count Arthur Strong's Radio Show* by Steve Delaney. After seven radio series and a Sony Radio Academy Award, the bumbling former variety star from Doncaster got a six-part series on BBC Two. Writer and comedian Jason Byrne's fast-paced Radio 2 sitcom *Father*

Figure, in which he plays a disastrous house-husband, has also become a six-part series on BBC One.

The competition for the comedy slots is intense. Jane Berthoud, head of BBC Radio Comedy, says 'there is a temptation to place radio comedy in remarkable situations or places, because you can'. She advises writers to start with characters and write from their own experience. She quotes as a good example Justin Moorhouse, a stand-up comic from Manchester, who wrote *Everyone Quite Likes Justin*. The series is all about his comedy and social disasters, which is why Jane thinks it is particularly successful. She also mentions *On the Hour*, which started on radio parodying current affairs broadcasting. Written by Chris Morris, Armando Iannucci, Steven Wells, Andrew Glover, Stewart Lee, Richard Herring and David Quantick, it launched Alan Partridge and moved to television as *The Day Today*. Jane attributes its success to the in-depth knowledge that its creators had about their characters. Steve Coogan knew where Alan Partridge was born. He even knew his middle name. As a result he and the team were able to come up with credible dialogue and scenes shot through with truths about the embarrassingly affable DJ.

In the 11.30 a.m. comedy slot on Radio 4, writers are encouraged to be 'edgy but not smutty'. The commissioning editor looks for a plot or structure that makes it easy for listeners to follow and characters and situations that are rooted in reality that the audience will recognise and quickly engage with. They don't want surreal or complex pieces here. A good example is *Fags, Mags and Bags* by Sanjeev Kohli and Donald McLeary. Set in a Glasgow corner shop, the staff of Fags, Mags and Bags are tireless in their quest to bring nice-price Custard Creams and cans of Coke with Arabic writing on them to an ungrateful nation. Ramesh Majhu is the man who runs the shop, ably assisted by Dave and un-ably assisted by his sons Alok and Sanjay. Like all good sitcoms, it's the characters the audience love. Father and sons are trapped in a tiny business struggling to survive, and the Scottish-Asian mix is inspired and original. The first series was nominated for a Sony Radio Academy Award and it won a Writers' Guild Award in November 2008 for Radio Comedy of the Year.

Radio 4 don't want topical comedy in the morning slot. They have plenty of that in programmes such as *The Now Show* written by Steve Punt and Hugh Dennis, broadcast at 6.30 p.m. And they don't want comedy crime, spoofs of television or radio programmes, or programmes about people working in the media or the arts. They already have two long-running popular series featuring arts workers: *Count Arthur Strong's Radio Show* and *Ed Reardon's Week* by Chris Douglas and Andrew Nickolds, a sitcom about a curmudgeonly fifty-something writer. Described in the show's publicity material as an 'author, pipe-smoker, consummate fare-dodger and master of the abusive email', he lives in genteel poverty with his cat, Elgar, scraping a living as a hack by working through commissions for coffee-table books such as Pet Peeves, a collection of celebrity pet anecdotes. Like *Count Arthur Strong's Radio Show*, this is also in its seventh series, so steer clear of sitcoms about writers and actors unless your idea is so radically different that it has to be heard.

In the late-night comedy slot at 11 p.m., Radio 4 commissioning editors want programmes 'that play with genre, form and sound in a clever and entertaining fashion for intelligent and curious listeners'. They are wary of monologues as this programme follows Book at Bedtime, a reading for a single voice. New writers are welcomed and all writers are encouraged to take a risk here. For example, *Down the Line,* by Charlie Higson and Paul Whitehouse, was a spoof phone-in with a very realistic sound and some edgy callers. In the first episode a right-wing 'England for the English' supporter, a teller of terrible jokes and an incredibly boring man, lay into host Gary Bellamy, urging him to take a tough line with his guests. Taking their advice Gary bullies a sensitive elderly lady until he makes her cry. It certainly was edgy. It made me squirm, but in a good way, and the first series got lots of complaints because listeners thought it was real. It briefly transferred to television but the idea was too firmly rooted in radio to work well there. *Down the Line* returned to Radio 4 in 2013, but in the more mainstream 6.30 p.m. slot.

The other thing to think about with comedy is that it is often under-represented in the drama slots, and a single drama could become the basis of a series. For example, in *The Kneebone Cadillac*, an afternoon comedy drama by Carl Grose (see extract in Part One, Chapter Five), the Kneebone family of St Day in Cornwall have hard lives, weird vehicles and a love of country and western music. When scrap dealer Jed Kneebone dies, his three children, Slick, Dwight and Maddy, are left in serious trouble. In an attempt to pay off a massive tax bill and stave off advances from some particularly nasty drug lords, Maddy enters her father's vintage Caddy in a stock car race. She doesn't win the prize money and the Caddy gets put through a crusher, but the siblings are briefly brought together. This wildly inventive comedy is the King Lear story in a modern guise, except this father bequeaths a pile of debts to his children and the characters are more Cornish than the crimp on a pasty. Radio 4 commissioned a follow-up series of five fifteen-minute dramas called *The Kneebone Bonanza*. Set a year later, we find the Kneebone siblings still in financial ruin and the house showing signs of serious subsidence, but everything changes when they discover an old family legacy, a lost gold mine in Arizona, which could hold the answer to their prayers. Carl Grose is an inspired comedy writer and I hope there will be more Kneebone sagas to come.

PART SIX

Notes on Dramatisations

STEPHEN

Dramatisations

A large percentage of BBC radio drama consists of dramatisations of existing works of fiction and (less frequently) non-fiction. 'Dramatised for radio' is now the description of choice rather than 'Adapted for radio', and in a way that's understandable. An adaptation could, for example, involve cutting and rearranging an existing text to fit a specific time slot, whereas a dramatisation clearly means that the writer has turned the book into a fully fledged radio drama.

There has always been the Classic Serial slot, an hour a week devoted to a dramatisation in several episodes of a 'classic', although the definition of a classic has changed quite considerably over the years. Dramatisations are also to be found quite frequently in the Saturday Drama and the Fifteen-Minute Drama slots, and even on occasion in the Afternoon Drama slot.

The biggest change in recent years is a much more fluid and inventive view of how dramatisations should be presented, challenging accepted notions of when and how they should be heard. The radio dramatisation has become an event. For example, Robin Brooks did a dramatisation of James Joyce's *Ulysses* for 'Bloomsday' (16th June) 2012 in which his dramatisation covering the whole work was presented in seven parts all on the one day. In 2011, Jonathan Myerson and Mike Walker created a version of Vasily Grossman's epic novel, *Life and Fate*, which centres round the bloody World War Two battle of Stalingrad. It lasted eight hours with its thirteen separate episodes spread across all the available drama slots for the week it was broadcast. Robert Forrest and Shaun McKenna created *The Complete George Smiley*, dramatising all eight of John le Carré's novels about his enigmatic spy hero, which again, over a period of time, were heard in both the Saturday Play and Classic Serial slots. Along with Robin Brooks, I worked on *Classic Chandler*, where, within the Saturday Play slot, we offered versions not just of the six well-known Philip Marlowe detective stories but also of his never-before-dramatised last novel and of a novel he started which was completed by somebody else – enough to satisfy the most completist Chandler fan.

Exciting and innovative work therefore is taking place in this area and there's no doubt dramatisations represent a very significant part of the output. Of course, the bad news for new writers is that it's very rare for writers without a track record to be given a chance to work on dramatisations. But then no one working inside radio drama would ever suggest that all this should be allowed to drown out the original work and the individual voice.

Looking at it from another angle, there is no doubt that you can learn a great deal about writing for radio from listening to dramatisations. Here are some of the things you might like to think about it while you're doing it.

1. Radio is the home of the word and therefore it has closer links to the novel, the short story and the poem than to television or film. It's possible therefore in a radio dramatisation to preserve something of the verbal quality of the original work – the delicately precise phrases of James Joyce, the sardonic asides of William Makepeace Thackeray, the witty physical descriptions of Raymond Chandler – in a way which is impossible in a visual medium. This is worth thinking about in your original work. The turn of phrase counts in a far more significant way than in television or film. Sometimes radio language can have the precision and grace of poetry.

2. It's very common in dramatisations to use a narrator. With a Charles Dickens or a Henry Fielding novel it becomes possible to bring the author into the aural picture as controllers and commentators on their own narratives. Fielding in *Tom Jones,* for example, plays games all the time with the reader and adds mock-heroic prefatory chapters and commentaries, so there was an opportunity to bring some of this gusto into the listener's experience of a dramatisation. (We've given an imaginative example of how to handle a narrator of this sort in the extract from Charlotte Jones's dramatisation of Roald Dahl's *Matilda* in the Narrators chapter in Part One).

But this approach does not work for all dramatisations; there is no 'one size fits all', and a decision about who (if anybody) narrates the story is a crucially important one when it comes to working out how to handle adapting a book. Sometimes it's easy. After all, Raymond Chandler's Philip Marlowe is a wonderfully sardonic narrator in Chandler's books, full of world-weary asides and wonderful turns of phrases ('The subject was as easy to spot as a kangaroo in a dinner jacket'; 'Perfumes in little pastel phials tied with ducky satin bows, like little girls at a dancing class.') Why make life difficult for yourself when all that is available? Sometimes it's not. If the book is written in the third person, what is lost or gained by giving the narrative instead to the main character? I worked at one point on an adaptation of the wonderful Russian novel *Oblomov,* by Ivan Goncharov, written in the mid-nineteenth century, about a man who is so exquisitely sensitive and aware that he ends up putting off every decision in his life and taking to his bed. He becomes the ultimate couch potato because he simply cannot cope with the world. The novel is told in the third person and there are a number of scenes in it where Oblomov himself does not appear. But I had an instinct that it would work better for the dramatisation if we were inside Oblomov's head, sharing his anxieties and worrying with him about his endless ability to put things off. So certain scenes had to go, but the dramatisation (I hope) acquired a focus it might not otherwise have had. Instead of judging him, we identified with him.

The issues we've talked about in relation to original drama apply to *all* radio drama.

3. If you ever get the chance to listen to the radio dramatisation of a book you know well, then do it. Indeed, I'd go so far as to say it would be worth reading (or re-reading) a book ahead of listening to the radio version so that you can think about the decisions which have been made, what's been left out, what's been expanded, which characters have been cut, which bits of the plot have been simplified (or, very rarely, complicated.) Because this is a very useful way of thinking about radio storytelling and how it works. If you question the decisions that were made, then ask yourself how you would have handled it differently. If you like the changes, then why have they been made and why do they work? Because, although a radio dramatisation is based on an existing work, it has a life of its own. Or it should in order to justify its existence. If you feel a dramatisation has diminished a work you love then it has in some way failed. If it has opened new doors or hit you with the force of an original work then it's earned its keep.

Comparing a work you know with a radio version is certainly a helpful way of thinking through the issues we've been looking at. And maybe you'll be doing your own dramatisations in the future.

The Talented Mr Ripley

Some years ago, I did a dramatisation of Patricia Highsmith's novel, *The Talented Mr Ripley*, directed by Claire. It was the first in a series of five Saturday Dramas collectively given the title *The Complete Ripley* because they represented the first time that all five novels, which Highsmith had created over a period of nearly twenty years about her anti-hero, Tom Ripley, had been brought together and dramatised as a group.

Ripley is a psychopath who lies, cheats and murders, but Highsmith, writing in the third person, still tells the story from his point of view, seducing us into collaborating with Tom and wanting him to get away with every murder and every cheat. So one basic decision we made was very simple and as it turned out very effective. Ripley became our narrator. Which in radio means that we naturally get drawn into his way of seeing things and the events that happen are experienced as he views them. Spending time inside Tom Ripley's head is very disturbing, which is exactly how it should be.

But here the fun starts. The dramatisation was commissioned at sixty minutes. In its final transmitted form that's around 10,000 words. Patricia Highsmith's original novel, published in 1955, which is driven by plot rather than by introspection, is more than 100,000 words. That means in practical terms that, including all stage directions and character names, I had roughly ten per cent of the original to tell the story. And, bear in mind, things often move slower in sound than in prose. The statement 'He hit him and he staggered back' translates into an audio sequence that is going to take a lot lot longer.

And here's a further complication. The hook of *The Talented Mr Ripley* is that Tom murders his rich friend,

Dickie Greenleaf, and then successfully forges a will which allows him a life of luxury at Dickie's expense. This is the story which sets up and explains the four novels which are to follow, which show Ripley living at his financial ease in the South of France. So unless the listener understands where Tom is coming from and how he comes to kill Dickie, the whole series may as well pack up its bags and go home. I had to jettison most of the material about Tom's early life in order to start with the point at which Dickie's father, who assumes Tom knows Dickie better than he does, asks him to go over to Italy to see what Dickie's up to. I had to cut most of the things that happen on the ocean liner from America to Europe (regular aeroplane flights were still in their infancy) and then deliver Tom into Italy and make him link up with Dickie and his on/off girlfriend, Marge. We know nothing about Tom's sexuality but there's something disturbing going on. Finally after an on/off battle between Marge and Tom for Dickie's affections, Tom, who has lost out, persuades Dickie to go on a last trip together. The homoerotic subtext is not spelled out (nor was it in the dramatisation) though it's undoubtedly there. In a wild sudden moment of fury Ripley beats Dickie to death. And then starts to work out what to do next.

This is absolutely the core of the Ripley books; it's the first release of Tom's psychopathic violence. It sets up the sexual ambiguity, the reason for Tom's later wealth, the reason why people turn up pursuing Tom with questions about what he did and didn't do to inherit Dickie's money. There was no doubt that this had to be done well and convincingly. Otherwise nothing afterwards would make any sense.

All well and good but, even with the short cuts I'd decided on and described above, by the time the murder had taken place, I was thirty-five minutes into my sixty-minute dramatisation and on something like page ninety (in the Penguin edition) of a 240-page book. The pacing felt right and there was nothing more I felt I could omit in the build-up to the murder. But the result was that the proportions of the story had drastically altered. Basically the decisions I'd made had already defined the story I was going to tell, apologies to Patricia Highsmith.

A second murder committed by Ripley to cover up his first murder ended up being cut completely. (If you've seen the Anthony Minghella screen version lasting 130 minutes, you'll see why the murder of the character played by Philip Seymour Hoffman is actually potentially quite powerful.) By the time I'd written fifty-five minutes of the script, I was somewhere about page 180 in the novel. I ended up creating a scene in a bar between Ripley, Marge and Dickie's father, lasting about three to four minutes, which summarised the denouement in which Marge backtracked on her suspicions and Tom got his inheritance. Oh, and the last sixty pages of the novel.

Of course, you need to know a book well before you start writing a dramatisation. You need to break down its plot into various stages so you understand what is and is not important. Personally, I always do a chapter-by-chapter summary to let me see how the book is set out – and also to identify what is and is not important in story and character terms.

But basically, at the end, you're still your own storyteller. You have to tell the story which is developing, not the story you thought you were going to tell which was faithful to the novel. Others may well do it differently but I try to write a dramatisation as if it was my own story and I don't know what's going to happen next. Over-planning is death. You have to choose what seems to you important and go with it. Sometimes you have to go back because you hadn't set something up properly. Sometimes you realise that a long scene you thought was very important isn't important at all. And always the clock is ticking away because, in radio terms, you only have a very limited and precise length of time to tell your story.

One other point: never be tempted to dramatise a book you don't really like or respect. If you don't feel some affinity with the material, then you're not very likely to do a good job. Again, the question isn't whether the book is a 'good' or 'well-written' one, it's whether you want to spend a significant amount of time absorbing and transforming that particular author's imaginative vision. Thomas Hardy, for example, is a highly regarded author, whose works make effective and popular radio dramatisations. But I find much of his work ponderous and humourless so I'm not the person who should ever agree to tackle *Jude the Obscure* or *Tess of the D'Urbervilles*.

PART SEVEN

Notes on Drama-documentaries

CLAIRE

Drama-documentaries

Drama-documentaries can be found in almost any drama slot. They are not commissioned in great numbers because they are not offered in anything like the volume of other kinds of drama. In drama-documentaries, fictional scenes are structured around interviews, archive recordings or written material such as diaries, biographies, letters or poetry. Working on a drama-documentary can be enormously time-consuming as the writer and producer have to gather and incorporate documentary extracts into a play without losing sight of the drama. The danger is that documentary interviews can be so riveting that the drama sounds flat or the other way round, particularly if the interview material has been recorded in less than ideal conditions. I have certainly made this mistake myself. But the upside is that, by mixing actors with actuality, you can get a distinctive sound and give your story lots of extra authenticity. If you are a journalist or from a programme-making background, this could be the genre for you.

An outstandingly good example of a drama-documentary is *Blasphemy and the Governor of Punjab*, broadcast in Radio 4's Saturday Drama slot and written and directed by John Dryden. On 4th January 2011, self-made millionaire businessman and governor of Punjab, Salmaan Taseer, was gunned down in the car park of a popular Islamabad market. He had been leading a campaign to amend Pakistan's blasphemy laws, after an illiterate Christian woman from a village in his province had been sentenced to death for blasphemy. Journalist and presenter Owen Bennett-Jones used interviews with the governor's family and friends and the family of the assassin, as well as reconstructions, to build a modern murder story that was both astonishing and thoroughly depressing. Taseer's killer was fêted across Pakistan. Lawyers offered to take his case for free and he is still deemed a hero. The play was compelling and revealing about modern Pakistan and the drama and documentary worked seamlessly together. I felt as if I was actually there.

Drama-docs don't have to be about hard-hitting political subjects. In *Like an Angel Passing Through My Room,* writer Christopher Green secured an exclusive interview with the very private Anni-Frid Lyngstad, aka Frida from the band Abba. Her reflections on being an object of adoration for millions were intercut with events from Christopher's life as her devoted fan. This project was several years in the making. Christopher's partner died shortly after we recorded the interview with Frida and, in their conversation, Frida had talked about her path to recovery after the death of her husband. What started as an upbeat reflection on fame developed into a meditation between two people dealing with life's blows. This drama-documentary for the Afternoon Drama slot was deeply personal and reflective but with a comic sensibility. I loved the mixture. It's a production that I am really proud to have worked on and we got to meet Frida from Abba!

An example of a different kind of drama-documentary is *Through the Wire* by Helen Macdonald, also for the Afternoon Drama slot. This was about British POWs in German camps in World War Two, who kept themselves sane by studying the birds that flew freely around them. Using scientific papers, monographs, letters and diary entries, Helen created a drama about men sitting still and carefully recording birdlife. Three of the prisoners addressed us directly and we heard extracts from their detailed bird observations. Their voices were occasionally intercut with a female narrator who told us who was who, and what eventually happened to them. We learnt that John Buxton's monograph on the redstart, based on his observations in the camps, has become a classic, and Peter Conder later became the Director of the Royal Society for the Protection of Birds. It was an unusual POW story, quietly moving and told very simply. Using the extracts from the men's personal recordings gave the play authenticity.

In order to get a drama-documentary commissioned you and your producer have to be clear in the proposal about exactly what the documentary element will give the listeners; in other words, what this approach has that a straightforward dramatisation of the story does not. If you are a journalist or have experience of making documentaries for television or film, that could also help you get this kind of commission.

Researching real-life stories can be fascinating. You are usually tapping into subjects or events that people feel passionately about, which makes for great listening. As with other kinds of drama, your producer will advise you about getting the rights to use published material or getting permission to interview someone. Rights are ultimately the producer's responsibility. Although recording equipment is quite simple to use, unless you are used to recording interviewees I wouldn't advise you to do this yourself. Go with your producer. It can be an advantage if one of you concentrates on the recording while the other focuses on the questions.

I produced *Underground*, a drama-documentary about the last tin mine in Cornwall, with writer Nick Darke. I interviewed miners, looking for a range of voices and experiences, trying to judge beforehand on the phone if they would be good talkers. Nick wasn't going to be with me. He was going to listen to the interviews in order to write a drama around them. If you are doing the interviewing it is important to take your time, listen carefully and avoid jumping in at the end of an answer. Let the moment happen. I tried to ask questions which would provoke a story and avoid ones to which there could be a 'yes' or 'no' answer. I also made sure my questions could be cut out so Nick could insert the selected clips cleanly into the drama. A good final question which I used at the end of each interview was 'is there anything that you would like to say that we haven't covered?' This almost always produced something interesting and unexpected. I also recorded at least a minute of atmosphere in the interview space (with no speech), which was useful later to edit smoothly in and out of the clips.

Nick and I worked closely together to choose exactly the right extracts and Nick wrote a drama about two men on their final shift on the last working day in South Crofty, which was intercut with actual miners talking about their work, their community and their way of life. The pride the miners took in their work was inspiring. It's a world the rest of us could never experience and it was about to disappear for ever. The interview clips then had to be transcribed and included in the script so the sound engineer knew how to assemble the production.

Unlike other kinds of drama, the writer of a drama-doc is often involved in the editing process, as the clips are refined and embedded in the drama. The producer and writer work closely together throughout. Drama-documentaries can be labour intensive but the sheer variety of stories that real people have to tell, and the quality of their voices, can make this an immensely rewarding genre to work in.

PART EIGHT

Landmark Radio Drama

CLAIRE

If you want to appreciate the scope of radio drama just listen to, or read, these six landmark plays. Each of them was groundbreaking in its own way and each of them has had a lasting influence on the art form. I have also chosen them because they are all readily available online in audio form and from booksellers. They constitute to some extent a history of the genre, but in re-listening to them I was struck by how contemporary they sound.

The War of the Worlds by H.G. Wells, adapted by Howard Koch and Orson Welles

First broadcast on CBS the day before Hallowe'en, 30th October 1938, *The War of the Worlds* was directed and narrated by Orson Welles. You may know the film but if you've never heard the original radio drama then it's really worth a listen. Vital, convincing and spine-chilling, the first two thirds of the sixty-minute broadcast is a series of simulated news bulletins, which suggested to many listeners that an actual alien invasion by Martians was taking place.

The introduction to the broadcast clearly stated that it was based on H.G. Wells's novel, but many people hadn't heard the programme from the start. On that night audiences were told they were listening to the music of Ramon Raquello and his Orchestra, live from New York's Hotel Park Plaza. In reality, the orchestra was playing in a CBS studio. The dance music was interrupted by a series of increasingly alarming simulated news bulletins. An astronomer, played by Welles, commented on reports that several explosions of 'incandescent gas' had been observed on the planet Mars. Then a news bulletin reported that a huge flaming object had struck a farm in New Jersey and it cut to a journalist at the scene, who described seeing an alien crawl out of a spacecraft. 'Good heavens, something's wriggling out of the shadow. It glistens like wet leather. But that face. It... it is indescribable.' The alien invasion was underway and by the end of the first half of the programme the radio studios themselves were under attack. The production company, Mercury Theatre on the Air, founded by John Houseman and Orson Welles, ran their regular drama slot without commercial breaks, which added to the programme's realism.

Thousands of people, believing they were actually being invaded by Martians, flooded newspaper offices and radio and police stations with calls. Panicked listeners packed roads, hid in cellars, and loaded their guns. According to *The New York Times*, in one block of Newark, New Jersey, twenty families rushed out of their houses with wet towels over their faces as protection from Martian poison gas.

In 1938, with the world on the brink of World War Two, audiences were already anxious. The breaking-news format used in *The War of the Worlds* echoed the radio coverage of the Munich crisis only a month before. But it is likely that newspaper accounts over the following week exaggerated the hysteria because they were resentful of their radio news rivals. There are estimates that about twenty per cent of those listening believed it was real. That translates as less than a million people.

Orson Welles knew how to use radio's imaginative possibilities and he was a master at blurring the lines between fiction and reality. The recording is crackly and ancient-sounding but it moves incredibly swiftly and is an enthralling piece of storytelling. The fact that none of it was pre-recorded and that it was all created so convincingly 'live' on that night is a truly astonishing technical feat. According to *The New York Times*, Welles expressed profound regret that his dramatic efforts should have caused consternation. 'I don't think we will choose anything like this again,' he said, but the episode made him world famous.

I thought of *The War of the Worlds* when a miniature furore broke out around *Down the Line* by Paul Whitehouse and Charlie Higson. Radio 4 listeners thought the late-night spoof phone-in was real, and even when they discovered it was not, some were furious that they had been deceived. It just goes to show that, over seventy years after *The War of the Worlds* was first broadcast, radio still holds an incredibly powerful sway over its audiences.

Under Milk Wood by Dylan Thomas

The BBC first broadcast *Under Milk Wood: A Play for Voices*, starring Richard Burton, on the Third Programme on 25th January 1954, two months after Dylan Thomas's death. A repeat was broadcast two days later. Daniel Jones, the Welsh composer who was a lifelong friend of Thomas's and his literary trustee, wrote the music. The play won the Prix Italia Award for Radio Drama that year. In the first recording, several sections were omitted. The complete play was recorded and broadcast in 1963 and it was later adapted into a stage play and a film.

In *Under Milk Wood*, the narrator (Burton) invites the audience to listen to a day in the life of fictional Welsh fishing village Llareggub ('bugger all' backwards). We hear the dreams and innermost thoughts of the inhabitants including: Mrs Ogmore-Pritchard, relentlessly nagging her two dead husbands; Captain Cat, reliving his seafaring times; the two Mrs Dai Breads; Organ Morgan, obsessed with his music; and Polly Garter, pining for her dead lover.

Starting life several years earlier as a short story, the play had its first reading in May 1953 in New York at The Poetry Center. Dylan Thomas narrated. Almost as an afterthought the performance was recorded and later issued by the Caedmon Company.

What's groundbreaking about it? Richard Burton puts in an outstanding performance as the narrator with every syllable nuanced to perfection, but the main star of the piece is Dylan Thomas's wonderful language. Words of such depth, lilt and lyrical rhythm that they take your breath away, and Burton takes the narration at quite a pace by today's standards. The Welsh voices are rich and authentic and must have been particularly distinctive in an era when everyone in broadcasting sounded like the Queen. And this is about the lives of ordinary people as they awake, perform their daily tasks, socialise, gossip, and daydream about the past that might have been and the future that may still hold hope. Polly Garter, with her numerous children by different fathers, dreams of Willie, a very small man who was the love of her life. Captain Cat, the blind bell-ringer, thinks of all the sailors he knew who died at sea. Mr Pugh dreams of poisoning his wife, and young Gwenny, who has extorted pennies from the little boys who do not want to kiss her, plans for the next day and more pennies. There are powerful, often sexual, forces operating beneath the calm exterior of a town which has 'fallen head over bells in love'. Each relationship is governed by peculiar rules but each of the characters remains deeply involved in his or her own idea of love. In Thomas's world, these sensuous relationships are closely linked to the idea of death.

The sound effects are simple: a cock's crow, barking dogs, the sea, bell buoys. And music adds to the sense of character and place: a mournful tune performed by Polly Garter in a minor key, as she remembers Willie and compares him to her other lovers, a children's singing game or little Gwenny's cheeky song to three very young boys.

Under Milk Wood is often parodied and has given rise to a host of imitators. Annamaria Murphy wrote her play *Rosie's Beauty* as a homage to it. I bought a cheap CD of it online and sat in the dark for ninety minutes as the warm bath of words flowed over me. You can even hear Richard Burton rustling his script – they obviously didn't care about that sort of thing in those days. A completely entrancing listen.

Albert's Bridge by Tom Stoppard

First broadcast by the BBC on 13th July 1967 starring John Hurt, *Albert's Bridge* was the first full-length play that Stoppard wrote for the radio. In 1968, it won an award at the Czechoslovak International Radio Play Festival, held in Prague. In Rome, it won the Prix Italia, an international award for the best radio play. The play was re-recorded in 1988 with Paul Copley as Albert.

It is about a young man with a philosophy degree who is employed with three others to paint a huge road bridge. It takes them two years to paint the entire bridge, at which point they must begin again because the paint only has a lifetime of two years. Albert claims that he can paint the bridge all by himself using paint with a lifetime of eight years. Albert loves the bridge. He rejects a job in manufacturing offered to him by his father and finds peace of mind high up among the geometrically ordered bridge girders, away from the demands of his wife and child.

Albert gets the job, the other painters are sacked and he meets Frazer, a potential suicide, who climbs the bridge only to discover, once he has escaped the pressure of life below, that he no longer wants to jump, so he repeatedly ascends and descends.

Albert is obsessed with order. He refuses to even take a holiday. His wife leaves him and, in spite of his efforts, after two years the bridge collapses when 1,800 painters march on it without breaking step; an excess of order on a physical level.

So what's groundbreaking about this play? This is an early example of the work of a major British playwright. Radio was of crucial importance in the development of Tom Stoppard's career. His original plays for radio form a large part of his non-theatre work. It is a political satire, which was unusual in radio plays at that time; the absurdities of the council's decisions are hilarious. The passions and concerns of an ordinary man are shot through with abstract ideas. Albert is surrounded by robust working-class voices and, although he is in some ways a pitiable Chaplinesque figure, Tom Stoppard makes you really care about him.

The Hitchhiker's Guide to the Galaxy by Douglas Adams

The first radio series was broadcast in 1978 on BBC Radio 4 and, despite a low-key launch, it received a tremendous audience reaction. It was repeated twice in 1978 alone. This led to an LP re-recording, produced independently of the BBC, and a further adaptation of the series as a book. A second radio series was broadcast in 1980.

What started as a science fiction comedy for radio blossomed into an international multimedia phenomenon. There have been stage shows, a 'trilogy' of five books published between 1979 and 1992, a sixth novel penned by Eoin Colfer in 2009, a 1981 television series, a 1984 computer game and three series of three-part comic book adaptations of the first three novels published by *DC Comics* between 1993 and 1996. A Hollywood-funded film version, produced and filmed in the UK, was released in April 2005, and radio adaptations of the third, fourth, and fifth novels were broadcast from 2004 to 2005. Many of these adaptations, including the novels, the television series, the computer game, and the earliest drafts of the Hollywood film's screenplay, were done by Adams himself, and some of the stage shows introduced new material written by Adams.

In the series we follow the adventures of Arthur Dent, a hapless Englishman, and Ford Prefect, an alien who named himself after the Ford Prefect car to blend in with what he assumed to be the Earth's dominant life form. Ford is from a small planet somewhere in the vicinity of Betelgeuse and a researcher for the eponymous guidebook. Then there is Zaphod Beeblebrox, Ford's semi-cousin and Galactic President, the depressed robot Marvin the Paranoid Android and Trillian, formerly known as Tricia McMillan, a woman Arthur once met at a party in Islington and the only other human survivor of Earth's destruction.

The first radio series came from a proposal called *The Ends of the Earth*, six self-contained episodes, all ending with the Earth being destroyed in a different way. While writing the first episode, Adams realised that he needed someone on the planet who was an alien to provide some context, and that this alien needed a reason to be there. Adams finally settled on making the alien a roving researcher for a 'wholly remarkable book' named *The Hitchhiker's Guide to the Galaxy*, and hearing extracts from the book became a crucial part of telling the story. The book, played by Peter Jones, gives the characters solid earthly advice on how to interpret the surreal and shifting universe in which they find themselves.

What's groundbreaking about it? Its surreal imagery and wordplay, mixing the ordinary with the fantastical, has had a huge influence on radio writing, particularly comedy, ever since. Much of the budget was spent on sound effects. Adams said that he wanted the programme's production values to be comparable to that of a modern rock album. It became cult listening, a cool club to be part of, and still has a huge number of die-hard fans all over the world who not only tuned in but bought the merchandise. It was the first comedy series to be produced in stereo and the later series of *Hitchhiker's* became some of the first radio shows to be mixed into four-channel Dolby Surround Sound. This was the comedy show which took radio listening into the rock era.

Cigarettes and Chocolate by Anthony Minghella

Anthony Minghella's sixty-minute drama, starring Juliet Stevenson, Bill Nighy and Jenny Howe, was broadcast on BBC Radio 4 in 1988 and won the Giles Cooper Award for Best Radio Play. It was revived on 3rd May 2008 as a tribute to its author following his death. *Cigarettes and Chocolate* was his second radio play, written at a point where his stage play *Whale Music* had been successful and he was working in television but had not yet received international recognition. Minghella went on to win a host of writing and directorial awards for the films *The English Patient*, *The Talented Mr Riley* and *Truly Madly Deeply*, and he returned to radio drama in 2006 with *Eyes Down Looking* on BBC Radio 3, starring Jude Law, Juliet Stevenson and David Threlfall, to mark Samuel Beckett's 100th birthday celebrations.

Cigarettes and Chocolate is the story of a young woman's dysfunctional relationships and the successful but empty world she inhabits. It opens with Gemma's family and friends leaving an increasingly anxious stream of messages on her answerphone. A friend wants her to go flat hunting, a lover wants to make a 'visit' and other friends and family wonder why she is not ringing them back. There is a lot of initial tension surrounding her whereabouts. Has she been killed or kidnapped? We listen to the phone messages for clues. Then she speaks and we begin to hear and assess the messages in a different way.

Because her friends can only hold a one-sided conversation they almost inevitably end up making some sort of confession to her, and Gemma becomes a silent witness to their shortcomings. We learn that the flat-hunting friend is pregnant but is also in emotional turmoil as the father seems unwilling to support her, her friend's husband is in love with her and her boyfriend is also sleeping with another of her best friends. All Gemma wants to do is sit at home with her cat and listen to Bach's *Matthew Passion* over and over again, and we begin to understand why.

An almost non-speaking central character is a very bold choice in a radio play. It's a bit like the exercise in an art class where you draw the space around an object rather than the object itself. The effect is to make the other characters' speeches urgent, intimate and often bleakly comic as they struggle to justify their behavior to the silent Gemma. Their voices are unrelieved by the sound of footsteps, doors or traffic. Their words tumble out as they race to fill the silence. The title derives from Gemma's repeated attempts to cope with the world. At first she tried cigarettes and then chocolate but discovers in the end that silence is the best method.

And the characters speak in intercutting monologues; at no point do they interact with each other. This is another unusual choice by Anthony Minghella. They are unreliable narrators of their own stories but we hear clearly what they are not saying: the lies, the self-deceptions and petty betrayals. The effect is to give us a close-up portrait of each of them and we gradually come to understand why Gemma has withdrawn from the world. She speaks only twice and then directly to the audience, not to her anxious friends and family.

Written during the rampant materialism of the Thatcher years, it is an exquisite insight into one young woman's quest for spiritual meaning. It also raises some interesting questions about speech, silence, and words in general. Minghella's play tells a good story but it is also an eloquent exploration of the fundamental limitations of spoken language. His characters talk a lot while actually saying very little. This irony is part of the point of this groundbreaking play: that verbal communication is at once impossibly flawed, and utterly vital. And where better to say this than on radio, where the word is all there is.

Spoonface Steinberg by Lee Hall

Spoonface Steinberg, a monologue for a seven-year-old child, was first broadcast on BBC Radio 4 on Monday 27th January 1997, produced by Kate Rowland. Such was the popular acclaim that the BBC repeated it the following Saturday afternoon and it sold thousands of copies on cassette. Becky Simpson won two awards for her performance. The play launched Lee Hall's playwriting career. It was voted one of the ten best radio dramas of all time by readers of the *Radio Times*. As Hall has since remarked: 'People remember where they were when they first heard Spoonface.' He went on to adapt *Spoonface Steinberg* for television and for the stage, and the play transferred to the West End in 2000.

On the face of it, Hall's play is probably one of the most daunting pieces imaginable, both for actor and audience: an hour-long monologue in which a seven-year-old autistic Jewish girl who is dying from cancer dreams of being a little bird floating up to heaven. But don't let this put you off. There isn't a whiff of mawkishness about Hall's hallucinatory, lyrical writing. Spoonface, so-called because of her perfectly round features, is trying to get a handle on life just as she is going to have to leave it. She does this by questioning and investigating her world, including her quarrelling parents and the cleaning lady, and revels in operatic death arias hoping, like 'the opera ladies', to die beautifully. The magic of something like this is always going to be in the language. With its avoidance of contractions, 'did not', 'I have', 'would not', etc., and various other verbal tics, Hall creates a sort of magic-realist patois unique to the central character. And who's to say what's realistic speech for an autistic seven-year-old anyway?

What the media said about the radio production:

> 'A truck driver confessed that the dramatic
> monologue *Spoonface Steinberg*, read by eleven-year-
> old Becky Simpson, had reduced him to tears.
> Hospices and hospitals said it would be useful in their
> work with the sick and dying and their families.
> Spoonface finds strength in the singing of Maria
> Callas and teachings from *The Kaddish*. Hall avoids
> sentimentality by making Spoonface funny and brave.
> She discovers meaning in her suffering.' Digby
> Hildreth, *Sunday Times*

> Lee Hall spoke on Radio 4's *Kaleidoscope* about writing
> this monologue. He said he did it in a couple of days,
> just letting it pour out unchecked. 'The result was
> astonishing: intensely moving but somehow bearable,
> perhaps because the little girl spoke with an innate
> calm wisdom which rang true as a tuning fork. After
> hearing the play, an old lady phoned the producer,
> Kate Rowland, and thanked her for allaying her own
> fear of death.' Sue Gaisford, *Independent on Sunday*

> 'After Monday's *Spoonface Steinberg*, 150 people
> telephoned the BBC to thank them for the play. On
> Friday's *Feedback* Chris Dunkley reported 108 calls
> and Chris Searle said it had brought the biggest ever
> response on the *Pick of the Week* hotline. Spoonface,
> eyeing her world with a child's cold curiosity, hot
> apprehension and occasional misapprehension, finds
> she can pass beyond it all. She does it through music.
> This writer believes in music's power to transform.'
> Gillian Reynolds, *Daily Telegraph*

Hall has gone on to write many other plays both for radio
and theatre, including: the musical *Billy Elliot*, which won
four Olivier Awards in London and ten Tony Awards on
Broadway; *The Pitmen Painters*, which won the Evening
Standard Award for Best Play; and screenplays for several
very successful films including *Billy Elliot* (2000), *Pride and
Prejudice* (2005), and *War Horse* (2011).

*

I chose these six dramas because they all elicited a passionate and enthusiastic response from their audiences and they
are still referred to by listeners, even though most of them
were broadcast a very long time ago. Don't feel you have to
set out to write groundbreaking drama – it will probably
come back to bite you if you do – but if you find any of these
inspiring, that's great. Go and find out more.

Appendices

An Exercise in Cutting

Writing radio drama usually means working within a strict time constraint: forty-five minutes in the case of an Afternoon Drama. This can often involve having to edit your work quite substantially to meet the time limitations imposed by the schedule. We've included here an example of a scene which had to be heavily cut. You may find it helpful in thinking about cutting your own work and the ruthlessness which is sometimes needed.

In this scene from Stephen's forty-five-minute play *Gerontius*, produced by Pier Productions, John Henry Newman (played by Derek Jacobi) and his acolyte and admirer, Ambrose St John (played by Nick Boulton), who is some twenty years younger, are in Rome. The date is 1846. They have recently, after much spiritual soul-searching, left the Church of England and gone over to the Roman Catholic Church. They have just had an audience with the Pope and they discuss their future plans, plans which will contribute to Newman being made a Cardinal at the end of his long life.

The scene played well enough at the readthrough because my producer, Martin Jenkins, and I had a very strong cast; but it was clear even then that the play would need to be cut quite heavily. Of course, cutting can be done in the editing (and often is), but with cuts as big as these, it makes better sense to cut before rather than after recording.

First of all we give the uncut scene, which ran to 830 words.

Then the cut version, which was around 560 words, i.e. a third of the scene has been removed.

AN EXERCISE IN CUTTING

If you're interested, you might like to try cutting the longer version yourself before taking a look at the cutting decisions we made.

Uncut Version of Scene (830 Words)

ST JOHN:	We'll soon dry out. But it was worth it, wasn't it?
NEWMAN:	Oh yes. He was very welcoming, didn't you find?
ST JOHN:	And we have our gifts. Your oil painting of the Mater Dolorosa and my coronation medal.
NEWMAN:	Yes. (PAUSE) Shall we sit?
ST JOHN:	Are you unwell?
NEWMAN:	Just tired. Please – let's sit.
	(THEY SIT. PAUSE)
ST JOHN:	You're not disappointed?
NEWMAN:	By what?
ST JOHN:	By what His Holiness said.
NEWMAN:	Not at all. He was very gracious, very attentive.
ST JOHN:	Oh yes, but I sometimes think – (HE STOPS HIMSELF)
NEWMAN:	What?
ST JOHN:	(SLOWLY) That now they have you, they don't know what to do with you. You were a wonderful catch but now they don't seem to be able to settle on a role for you. With all your talents, there must be something.

NEWMAN: Of course. (PAUSE) That is what we have to consider. And I do mean 'we'. The whole community of souls who have taken this momentous step.

ST JOHN: The Holy Father would obviously like it if we became members of a religious order.

NEWMAN: Yes. But –

ST JOHN: But?

NEWMAN: I do not think that is what I seek. If I am honest, it would try my faith very much to take a vow of poverty.

ST JOHN: But you already have so little.

NEWMAN: Yes, but what I have I still value. Perhaps overmuch. Besides, I am too old to begin life again by becoming the instrument of others. I want to be somewhere which offers opportunities for learning and scholarship. I want to be involved in education. I want –

ST JOHN: And, of course, whatever you want, I should wish to be with you.

NEWMAN: (TOUCHED) Thank you. (PAUSE) I don't think the vow of celibacy has ever been a problem for me.

ST JOHN: Nor for me. Why –

NEWMAN: For better or worse, my Anglican colleagues have become married. Very much for the worse in the case of my friend, Keble. But since I was fifteen, I have known that my calling in life would require such a sacrifice as celibacy involved. I would never marry.

ST JOHN: I feel the same. Any doubts I had are over.
                    Why speak now?

NEWMAN: I don't know. I felt – a need.

ST JOHN: We have made our vows.

NEWMAN: Of course. But sometimes it's necessary to
                    revisit these things. It is a fearful thing to tie
                    yourself to one person for life.

ST JOHN: Is this some accusation against me?

NEWMAN: Not at all. Just a reminder that whatever
                    happens we will be part of a community and
                    it is in that spirit that we must make our
                    plans for the future.

ST JOHN: It is a rebuke.

NEWMAN: It is what the future holds. Of course, I want
                    this to be a project we enter into together.
                    But we cannot act upon our own.

ST JOHN: Nor do I think we should either.

NEWMAN: I've upset you?

ST JOHN: No.

NEWMAN: I know I have.

ST JOHN: Whatever you decide is right.

NEWMAN: (LIGHTLY) What a burden. (PAUSE) The
                    suggestion has been made that we should
                    establish an Oratory. There are many
                    advantages.

ST JOHN: I liked the Oratory here.

NEWMAN: I found it the most pleasing of all the fine
                    things in Rome. With its library and sets of

rooms, its quiet, scholarly atmosphere, it
reminded me of an Oxford college.

ST JOHN: High praise from you.

NEWMAN: You feel the same.

ST JOHN: (SLOWLY) Yes, I do.

NEWMAN: There is no reason why we cannot have our
own Oratory. Funds will have to be raised
but the Church will support us. We can be
scholars and teachers. Oratories are always
situated in towns so –

ST JOHN: So where are you thinking of?

NEWMAN: Birmingham, of course. That's where we
have been based. We are not at its centre
which is good for our own tranquillity. But
there is a vast manufacturing population
close by in need of spiritual inspiration and
support. There will be educational work as
well as theological work.

ST JOHN: I thought you would say London.

NEWMAN: Because that is where you would have
chosen?

ST JOHN: Far from it. I'm like you. I prefer the more
secluded, methodical life to the mad hustle
and bustle of a capital, be it London or
Rome. But I feared worldly advice here in
Rome would try and urge you otherwise.
(PAUSE) I would be much happier in
Birmingham.

NEWMAN: I am so glad.

ST JOHN: You feared I'd disagree with you?

NEWMAN: I feared you'd say you agree with me when
              you did not. But I can hear in your voice that
              is not the case.

ST JOHN: Of course some will say we are choosing a
              backwater and others will take our place in
              London.

NEWMAN: We can only do what is right for us.

              (END OF SCENE)

APPENDIX

Cut Version of Scene (560 Words)

ST JOHN: We'll soon dry out. But it was worth it, wasn't it?

NEWMAN: Oh yes. He was very welcoming, didn't you find?

ST JOHN: And we have our gifts. Your oil painting of the Mater Dolorosa and my coronation medal.

NEWMAN: Yes. (PAUSE) Shall we sit?

ST JOHN: Are you unwell?

NEWMAN: Just tired. Please – let's sit.

(THEY SIT. PAUSE)

ST JOHN: You're not disappointed?

NEWMAN: By what?

ST JOHN: By what His Holiness said.

NEWMAN: Not at all. He was very gracious, very attentive.

ST JOHN: Oh yes, but I sometimes think – (HE STOPS HIMSELF)

NEWMAN: What?

ST JOHN: (SLOWLY) That now they have you, they don't know what to do with you. You were a wonderful catch but now they don't seem to be able to settle on a role for you. With all your talents, there must be something.

NEWMAN: Of course. (PAUSE) That is what we have to consider. And I do mean 'we'. The whole community of souls who have taken this momentous step. I want to be somewhere which offers opportunities for learning and scholarship. I want to be involved in education. I want –

ST JOHN: And, of course, whatever you want, I should wish to be with you.

NEWMAN: (TOUCHED) Thank you. (PAUSE) I don't think celibacy has ever been a problem for me.

ST JOHN: Nor for me. Why –

NEWMAN: For better or worse, my Anglican colleagues have become married. Very much for the worse in the case of my friend, Keble. But since I was fifteen, I have known that my calling in life would require such a sacrifice as celibacy involved. I would never marry.

ST JOHN: I feel the same. Any doubts I had are over. Why speak now?

NEWMAN: I don't know. I felt – a need.

ST JOHN: We have made our vows.

NEWMAN: Of course. But sometimes it's necessary to revisit these things. It is a fearful thing to tie yourself to one person for life.

ST JOHN: Is this some accusation against me?

NEWMAN: Not at all. Just a reminder that whatever happens we will be part of a community and it is in that spirit that we must make our plans for the future.

ST JOHN: Whatever you decide is right.

NEWMAN: (LIGHTLY) What a burden. (PAUSE) The suggestion has been made that we should establish an Oratory. There are many advantages. Funds will have to be raised but the Church will support us. We can be scholars and teachers. Oratories are always situated in towns so –

ST JOHN: So where are you thinking of?

NEWMAN: Birmingham, of course. That's where we have been based. We are not at its centre which is good for our own tranquillity. But there is a vast manufacturing population close by in need of spiritual inspiration and support. There will be educational work as well as theological work.

ST JOHN: I thought you would say London.

NEWMAN: Because that is where you would have chosen?

ST JOHN: Far from it. I'm like you. I prefer the more secluded, methodical life to the mad hustle and bustle of a capital, be it London or Rome. I would be much happier in Birmingham.

NEWMAN: I am so glad.

ST JOHN: You feared I'd disagree with you?

NEWMAN: I feared you'd say you agree with me when you did not.

(END OF SCENE)

Script Samples

Memorials to the Missing by Stephen Wyatt

Memorials to the Missing was first broadcast on BBC Radio 4 in November 2007. It was made by Pier Productions and directed by Martin Jenkins. Anton Lesser played Fabian Ware. It won the Tinniswood Award for best radio drama script and Silver in the Sony Radio Academy Awards.

The play is about Fabian Ware and the creation of the Imperial War Graves Commission, the organisation he founded to commemorate the deaths of soldiers killed during the First World War. This work climaxed in the building of a Memorial to the Missing, designed by Edwin Lutyens and built on a site in Thiepval, in northern France. It bears the names of more than 72,000 officers and men of the United Kingdom and South African forces who died in the Somme sector before 20th March 1918 and have no known grave.

The script begins in the present with on-site recordings of visitors reading names off the columns of the Memorial.

Then the voices of three of the missing speak.

Then we are inside Fabian Ware's head.

Then we are at a banquet to celebrate the completion of the construction of the Memorial in 1932 at which Ware is speaking.

Then we are inside Ware's head again as he remembers the events that made him decide to take up what becomes his life's work.

Then we move to a battlefield in 1914. Ware encounters a young woman. Her dead brother tries to speak to her but neither she nor Ware can hear him.

Then we move to the beginning of a long exposition scene in which Ware explains his idea to General Macready. He's given three minutes to do it.

FX:	AFTER TITLES.
	VOICES READING FROM THE ROLL-CALL OF NAMES ON THE MEMORIAL AT THIEPVAL.
	THEN OVER THIS, WHISPERING VOICES:
ONE:	(NORTH COUNTRY) I was sixteen. Lied about my age, didn't I, so I could enlist. Wanted to serve my country. Do what's right. You know, become a hero. Fat chance. Cut to pieces in the first moments of the attack by a burst of machine-gun fire.
TWO:	(UPPER CLASS) I was twenty-three, just married, first child on the way. Still scrabbling around for a career. But my wife agreed that it was right for me to go. This shell burst – very close – that's all I can remember.
THREE:	(COCKNEY) I was thirty almost. Been working on the docks all my life. So I loved the excitement of being abroad and being one of the lads. 'Your advance will end the war.' That's what they told us. Perhaps it did. I'm not around to know.
ONE:	I'm one of the missing.

TWO:	I'm one of the missing.
THREE:	I'm one of the missing.
FX:	THE VOICES OF THE ROLL-CALL CONTINUE UNDER:
WARE:	(V.O.) *I do not see myself as a superstitious or overly religious man. But it seems that for most of my later life I have been haunted by these voices – the voices of the dead.*
FX:	CROSS-FADE INTO BUZZ OF EXPECTANT GUESTS.
	THEN A GAVEL. BANQUET, 1932.
TOASTMASTER:	My lords, ladies and gentlemen, pray silence for Major General Sir Fabian Ware, CMG, CB, KBE, KCVO.
FX:	HUSH FROM GUESTS AS WARE RISES.
WARE:	My lords, ladies and gentlemen, I have been asked tonight to say something of the work of the Imperial War Graves Commission with which I have had the honour to be associated since its inception during the latter days of the Great War. As we know, the losses were and still are almost beyond comprehension. Britain and her Dominions lost 975,399 dead. Many of them in unmarked graves in distant lands or lost for ever in the mud of Flanders. The task of recording their deaths and providing memorials fitting to such loss and such sacrifice has been the guiding principle behind all the Commission's work. Perhaps it's appropriate if I begin by saying

	something about the origins of the Commission. In the very early days of the War, I was involved in…
FX:	HIS VOICE STARTS TO FADE DURING THIS.
	TO BE REPLACED AGAIN BY WARE'S INNER VOICE, QUIETER, MORE THOUGHTFUL.
WARE:	(V.O.) *Speaking of it now it's very easy to make everything seem so planned and so inevitable. So easy to forget about the exhaustion that set in when I was tired of arguing with boneheaded officials. And to ignore the powerful voices who opposed what we were doing. Perhaps it's fortunate that I've always been better at providing solutions than asking questions.*
FX:	CUT BACK TO WARE AT THE BANQUET.
WARE:	When the Great War began, I was already forty-five. A newspaper editor no longer with a newspaper to edit. I was too old for active service and too young to stay at home and wait. So I volunteered for the ambulance service and was put in charge of the motley collection of private cars and drivers which became known as the Red Cross Mobile Unit. Our job was to search out the wounded and dying and bring them to wherever they could be cared for. But I soon began to feel that part of our work had to involve collecting evidence about the dead – who they were, where they had fallen and where they were being buried.

FX:	ADD IN 1910s-TYPE CAR OVER BUMPY ROAD COMING TO A HALT. DISTANT SHELLING.
	CUT TO FEET OVER GROUND. 1914.
WARE:	(V.O.) *I can still see it. Two small clumps of graves in the fields near Bethune. I was in the vicinity so I went to see what state they were in. There were probably no more than ten graves in all. Lying there among some battered vegetables. With makeshift crosses also battered and broken by the rain.*
FX:	AS THE FEET STOP, THE VOICE OF ONE OF THE DEAD.
JAMES:	(UPPER CLASS) I was just twenty-one. As I was already at university and good at sports, this meant I was officer material. Became a Second Lieutenant. My men were rough round the edges, ordinary working-class fellows. Never met men like that before. Never talked to them anyway. They were decent enough and willing I'll give them that. Brave too. So when my map-reading got us trapped in enemy fire, they stood their ground. They did their best to give me a decent burial. The ones who were left alive that is.
FX:	FOOTSTEPS APPROACHING OVER FIELD.
ALICE:	(YOUNG, REFINED) Excuse me, sir.
WARE:	Of course.

ALICE: I saw you arrive just now, you see, and start to study the graves and I – I'm probably being very foolish.

WARE: (POLITELY) I'm sure that's not the case, ma'am.

JAMES: Alice –

ALICE: It's just that the instructions were so very precise. That is Bethune over there, isn't it?

JAMES: (MORE URGENTLY) Alice –

WARE: Forgive me, ma'am, but I confess I'm rather concerned to see you here unaccompanied. This is hardly a place for a young woman to –

ALICE: Please don't concern yourself about that, sir. I have a driver waiting for me over there. My family knows that I am here. I am looking for the grave of my brother, James. Perhaps you know him? Second Lieutenant James Cheveley?

WARE: I'm afraid I never had the honour.

JAMES: I'm here, Alice.

ALICE: I talked to his comrades in his regiment. They were most kind. They gave me the particulars of the exact place where – where James is buried. He died a hero they told me. They even described the temporary wooden cross and the inscription they had written upon it. I'm sure they wouldn't deceive me.

WARE: I'm certain they wouldn't.

ALICE:	I'm glad you confirm my impression. You see, I was looking over there because I thought that was the place they had described. Over there beyond the tree. But now I'm confused.
JAMES:	I'm here, Alice. Remember the gold ring you gave me? I'm still wearing it.
ALICE:	(STRUGGLING) So perhaps they meant here where you are looking.
JAMES:	Look hard, Alice. I am here.
	(PAUSE)
ALICE:	But no – you can't make out any of the names here either.
WARE:	Sadly the rain has done its best to obliterate them.
JAMES:	They only had time to write my name and rank but they did their best.
ALICE:	What are these crosses made from?
WARE:	Whatever's to hand. This one looks like an old army ration box to me. And this one – well, it's some kind of shell case...
ALICE:	And that's it?
JAMES:	They did their best.
ALICE:	He was my only brother and the apple of the eye of my parents. Such a talented young man with a great future. I had so hoped to find the spot where he was buried.
JAMES:	That last afternoon, Alice, remember? When we went for a long walk and talked about all

the things we would do, all the places we would visit, when I came home.

ALICE: Somehow I'd imagined he'd have a proper grave like in the churchyard at home. That was doubtless very foolish of me. But I did think there would be more than – this.

WARE: We do what we can. But there are so many calls upon our time. I have already made one very simple practical proposal. Every man should be given a well-made cross with a painted inscription and a tarred base to stop the rot so –

ALICE: (CLOSE TO TEARS) I know I should understand your difficulties but – I cannot. But I'm sure we will find the body in the end. And when it's been located, my family will make arrangements for James to be taken back to England

JAMES: No, Alice, listen –

ALICE: He can then be buried appropriately with full honours in the family tomb.

JAMES: Alice, listen, I don't want that. These are my men. We died together. I never thought I'd think that but I do. I don't deserve special treatment. They were decent fellows.

WARE: I am sorry to have disappointed you. But the task is huge. I will try to make further enquiries and see if I can – Cheveley, you said?

ALICE: Oh, I don't blame you. You will probably think me very silly for being upset when I

	should be proud that he has given his life to defend his country but – but –
JAMES:	(SOFTLY) Alice – listen to me.
ALICE:	(BUT HER CONTROL FINALLY GOES) Oh, James, James, where are you?
JAMES:	Alice – please –
ALICE:	James, James, come back to me.
FX:	HER ANGUISHED CRIES ARE DROWNED OUT BY THE SOUND OF HEAVY SHELLFIRE. THEN FADE DOWN UNDER:
WARE:	(V.O.) *Was it then the voices first spoke to me? Was it then that I knew it was my responsibility to make sure they were remembered – each and every one of them equal in death? I don't know. In all the books I've ever read and all the pictures I've ever seen when someone has a vision it comes to them in a sudden blinding moment of revelation. Well, that's not been my experience. My vision was built laboriously bit by bit.*
FX:	CUT TO A DOOR BURSTING OPEN.
WARE:	(ENTERING) General Macready, forgive me.
MACREADY:	Good God, man. How dare you –
WARE:	Please – forgive me. I need to speak to you personally and your staff have not been cooperative. This was the only way.
FX:	DOOR SHUTS.

MACREADY: You must be Fabian Ware.

WARE: But how did –

MACREADY: (INTERRUPTING) No other civilian would beard a general in his office without an invitation.

WARE: I'm sorry.

MACREADY: I'm afraid your reputation precedes you sir. Do you seriously imagine that I am here to lend an ear to every bleeding heart who brings me some sorry tale of injustice? Most of us are here to fight a war.

WARE: The successful prosecution of the war is, of course, paramount and –

MACREADY: I'm glad you recognise that.

WARE: And I would be the first to admit that what I have to propose has nothing to do with its successful termination.

MACREADY: Well, that's honest at least. So – why must you see me?

WARE: Put simply, I believe it is vital that the Army maintains a thorough register of every single man who dies in action and ensures that every single grave is clearly marked.

MACREADY: They tell me that once you have a bee in your bonnet there is no stopping you.

WARE: I hope – I believe – this is more than a bee in my bonnet.

MACREADY: Does this mean the Red Cross isn't doing its job?

WARE: The Red Cross is doing a remarkable job in
                  appalling circumstances –

MACREADY: But?

WARE: I believe the Armed Forces have a moral
                  obligation to be involved in this as well.
                  Indeed I think the only possible way to
                  proceed is for the Army to take full
                  responsibility for this work.

                  (PAUSE)

MACREADY: Very well, Mr Ware. Sit down.

WARE: (SITTING) Thank you.

MACREADY: You have three minutes to tell me why as
                  Adjutant-General of the British Expeditionary
                  Force, I should bother with some scheme or
                  other you've dreamed up which won't help
                  us one jot to beat the Germans.

Party Animal by Stephen Wyatt

Party Animal was first broadcast as a Friday Play on BBC Radio 4 in 2003. It was directed by Claire Grove with Philip Jackson as Martin. The play was shortlisted for the first Tinniswood Awards in 2004.

A contemporary piece with a more straightforward narrative than *Memorials to the Missing,* its basic story is outlined in Part Two, Chapter Three: Getting Started. Martin is trying to make sense out of the death of his son, Josh, and the possibility that Josh may have been a gay prostitute.

In this opening section of the play, we're presented with Martin as a narrator telling us the sequence of events surrounding Josh's death. But he's also moving back and forth in time, between dream and reality, while the party noises keep in our heads the crucial party at which Josh died and what may have happened there.

FX:	LOUD PARTY MUSIC. OVER THIS ANIMATED CHAT PUNCTUATED BY BURSTS OF LOUD LAUGHTER. KEEP BUT FADE DOWN UNDER THE FOLLOWING:
MARTIN:	(V.O. EARLY FORTIES, LONDON ACCENT) *I keep dreaming about going to this party I was never invited to. The music is loud. Everybody's shouting. And everybody's laughing – all the time. Nobody notices me. But then I'm not supposed to be there, am I? I walk through room after room after room crammed full of hundreds of people laughing and shouting. Many of the faces look familiar from the telly or the newspapers. But they're all too busy talking to each other to notice*

> *me. But then I'm there to find just one
> person – and one person only.*

<u>FX:</u>	<u>A PHONE RINGING CUTS OFF THE PARTY NOISE.</u>
	<u>THE PHONE IS PICKED UP.</u>
MARTIN:	Hello?
JOSH:	Dad?
MARTIN:	Where the hell are you?
JOSH:	In London.
MARTIN:	I know that but where?
JOSH:	I've got my own flat now.
MARTIN:	First I've heard of it.
JOSH:	Dad –
MARTIN:	What's up?
JOSH:	Oh, come on, Dad –
MARTIN:	You only phone when you want something so what is it this time?
JOSH:	I need to talk.
MARTIN:	You choose your moments, don't you? I don't hear for you for months and then you phone when I'm up to my eyes and running late.
JOSH:	Sorry, Dad.
MARTIN:	It's easy for you. You don't have a business to run with two men off sick and the delivery side's going up the creek. Is it urgent?
JOSH:	I don't know. It's hard to explain.

MARTIN:	Okay, then how about phoning me this evening? I'll be in after nine, God willing. Can it wait till then? (PAUSE) Well?
JOSH:	No, that's cool. See you, Dad.
MARTIN:	Oh, and Josh –
FX:	BUT JOSH HAS RUNG OFF.
	CUT BACK TO PARTY NOISES.
MARTIN:	(V.O.) *Of course this party I go to in my dreams isn't always exactly the same. Sometimes they're telling stories about him. Or saying things you know would make sense if only you had the key. But they never look my way. And they all have glasses in their hand and I don't. So I just keep on walking. And sometimes I think I finally understand. Sometimes I feel this time it's going to make sense.* (PAUSE) *And once I even thought I'd caught a glimpse of him in the distance. But of course he'd vanished before I could get to him.*
FX:	AGAIN THE PHONE CUTS THE PARTY SOUNDS OFF.
MARTIN:	Yes?
LESLEY:	Martin – it's Lesley.
MARTIN:	(SLOWLY) Well, well… First our son, now you.
LESLEY:	Don't be like that – please –
MARTIN:	You want something? I never hear from either of you unless you do.

SCRIPT SAMPLES

LESLEY:	Martin – <u>please</u> ...
	(SHE STARTS TO CRY.)
MARTIN:	(AT SEA) What's the matter?
LESLEY:	It's Josh.
MARTIN:	What's he up to now? He phoned me yesterday morning. Said he was going to phone back. Didn't of course. Knew he must be in some trouble or other. Bloody typical. I told him –
LESLEY:	(BREAKING IN) Martin – he's dead.
MARTIN:	What did you say? (PAUSE) What did you say?
LESLEY:	He's dead.
FX:	<u>A LONG PAUSE THEN MARTIN'S NARRATIVE VOICE IN A QUIETER HOME ACOUSTIC.</u>
MARTIN:	(V.O.) *What do you do? What do you say? I could have been standing there for seconds – or minutes – or even hours – holding that stupid phone in my hand.*
LESLEY:	(ON THE PHONE) Can you hear me, Martin? Are you still there?
MARTIN:	(V.O.) *When he was four he climbed up a tree and he couldn't get down. I held out my arms and told him to jump into them. And he did. And he was safe and I held him and he smelled of oranges. But that was years ago. I hadn't even see him for eighteen months.*
	(PAUSE)

LESLEY: Have you understood what I've been telling you? (PAUSE) Martin? (PAUSE) Are you there?

MARTIN: Yes, I'm here.

LESLEY: (VOICE BREAKING) I just can't believe it.

MARTIN: Me neither.

FX: CUT BACK TO HOME ACOUSTIC.

MARTIN: (V.O.) *She talked on but none of it made any sense. Then she rang off – and still it didn't make sense. It couldn't be true. It just couldn't. This wasn't about my son – about Josh. It was a stupid mistake. She'd got it wrong. She was winding me up.* (PAUSE.) *Someone phoned from work to ask me something and that didn't make any sense either. I put the phone down on them.* (PAUSE) *There wasn't much booze in the house so in the end I went out to get myself a bottle of Scotch. The offie had newspapers by the counter. There was a picture on the front page which looked like Josh. Couldn't think what he might be doing there. But I bought the paper anyway and took it home along with the Scotch.*

FX: RUSTLE OF NEWSPAPER. TELLY ON IN BACKGROUND.

MARTIN: (V.O.) *I switched the telly on to fill the silence. And I read the paper and kept reading it. You'll know Brad Ashton if you know your football. He's managed half the teams in the first division and still going strong. Well, he and his wife had a silver wedding anniversary party. A big do, they took over some posh hotel in the West End and invited hundreds of guests. Wall-to-wall celebrities. And this boy who I knew, just knew, wasn't Josh had been there. Josh didn't go to parties in big hotels. Josh didn't know celebs. But the front page of this rag said that he'd been there.* (PAUSE) *And he'd died there. So I finally got it into my thick head. Lesley hadn't made it up. Josh was dead.*

(PAUSE. TELLY CONTINUES.)

Resources

BBC Writersroom www.bbc.co.uk/writersroom

This is the one essential resource for everyone who is interested in writing for the BBC. There's a special section about radio drama and it offers, among other things, a wide range of radio scripts available for download, step-by-step writing tips and the opportunity to submit a script and get feedback on it. There's information about competitions, events and writing opportunities, including details of Writersroom's own radio play competition. And the information is constantly updated so its reliability is second to none.

BBC Drama Departments

The largest Radio Drama Department is based in central London: Room 6015, Broadcasting House, London W1A 1AA

BBC Radio Comedy is based at: Grafton House, 379–381 Euston Road, London NW1 3AU

There are three other regional centres producing radio drama within England:

BBC Radio Birmingham, Level 9, The Mailbox, 102–108 Wharfside Street, Birmingham B1 1AY

BBC Radio Bristol, Room 17.3, Broadcasting House, Whiteladies Road, Bristol BS8 2LR

BBC Radio Manchester, 4th Floor, Dock House, Salford M50 2BH

Scotland, Wales and Northern Ireland have production centres in:

BBC Radio Scotland, Room 4.02, Pacific Quay, Glasgow G51 1DA

BBC Radio Wales, Room G008, Broadcasting House, Llantrisant Road, Llandaff, Cardiff CF5 2YQ

BBC Radio Belfast, Room 3.07, Blackstaff House, 62–66 Great Victoria Street, Belfast BT2 7BZ

Your local production centre is probably your most useful point of contact. You can find producers' names in the online drama credits on the BBC website or in the *Radio Times*. We have not put a list here because producers come and go over time. Your radio-drama diary should have the most up-to-date contacts.

If you prefer to contact a BBC producer by email then their address will be in the form 'firstname.surname@bbc.co.uk'.

And don't forget to check the BBC Writersroom website for competitions or schemes within your region.

Independent Production Companies

The following independent production companies may be interested in hearing from new radio writers.

Goldhawk www.goldhawk.eu

Woolyback Productions www.woolybackproductions.com

Holy Mountain Ltd www.holymountain.co.uk

Sparklab www.sparklabproductions.com

Sweet Talk Productions www.sweettalkproductions.co.uk

There are a couple of websites which give further information about the independents:

Independent Radio Drama Productions www.irdp.co.uk
This offers helpful articles about writing for radio but no longer has the resources to offer advice or reply to emails.

Radio Independents Group (*RIG*) www.radioindies.org
Members-only site which gives advice and listings of what's on air each week produced by the independent production companies.

Writers' Organisations

The Writers Guild of Great Britain
www.writersguild.org.uk

The Writers' Guild of Great Britain is the trade union representing writers in television, radio, theatre, books, poetry, film, online and video games. On the website you can find full details of the BBC Radio Drama Agreement, jointly negotiated by the Guild and the Society of Authors, which sets out the conditions and rates of pay for a radio commission from the BBC. There are also articles and interviews.

Candidate Membership, which entitles you to Guild publications and access to a free contract vetting service, is open to any writer who has not yet had a professional contract for writing in terms at or above the Writers' Guild minimum terms. The website gives fuller details.

The Society of Authors www.societyofauthors.net

The Society has been serving the interests of professional writers for more than a century. On the website, you'll also find full details of the terms and conditions of the standard BBC Radio Drama Agreement, as well as information on radio production etiquette, articles and interviews. You are eligible to join the Society as soon as you have been offered a contract. Details are on the website.

Competitions

BBC Writersroom

The BBC Writersroom website has an up-to-date list of playwriting competitions including their own and others such as Laugh Out Loud, The Writers Prize, 15 Minutes Live and Slung Low.

IdeasTap www.ideastap.com

IdeasTap is an arts charity set up to help young people at the start of their careers. They work in partnership with the BBC and have in the past run a radio-drama competition for writers and offered mentoring schemes for playwrights.

The World Service International Radio Playwriting Competition www.bbc.co.uk/worldserviceradio

This competition is for anyone resident outside Britain, to write a fifty-three-minute radio drama for up to six characters. It is run by the BBC World Service and the British Council in partnership with Commonwealth Writers and is now in its twenty-third year. There are two categories: one for writers with English as their first language and one for writers with English as their second language. The two winners will come to London and see their play made into a full radio production, which will then be broadcast on the BBC World Service. They will also each receive a £2,000 prize and there are certificates for runners-up. The play must be in English, unpublished and must not have been previously produced in any medium. Whether you're experienced, new, or somewhere in between, the World Service want to hear from you. To find out how to enter, look on their website. The website also contains useful hints and tips for writers including how to set out your script, creating rhythm and texture, using sound in your play and writing in a second language. There are also brief interviews with experienced writers such as award-winning Nick Warburton and competition judge Roy Williams.

Courses

The Creative Skillset Media Academy Network
www.courses.creativeskillset.org/courses

A national network of colleges and universities that work with industry to develop media talent.

The Arvon Foundation www.arvonfoundation.org

A charitable organisation that runs residential creative-writing courses for schools, groups and individuals – including regular courses on writing for radio.

Other organisations such as *New Writing South*, *The University of Edinburgh* and *The Society of Authors* sometimes offer one-day or short courses but there's no regular pattern to this and all you can do is keep searching online.

Publications

Radio Times

Still the best resource for finding out what radio drama is going out and when. Unlike newspaper listings, it still gives writer, cast and producer credits.

Writers' & Artists' Yearbook and *Writer's Handbook*

Both publications contain listings for radio-drama contacts, both within the BBC and the independents, plus listings for writers' agents and articles relating to the business of writing.

If you're interested in finding out more about radio drama's distinguished early history, the standard study is *The History of Broadcasting in the United Kingdom* by Asa Briggs, published in five volumes by Oxford University Press. More specifically, the early history of radio drama is discussed in Alan Beck's 'The Invisible Play: BBC Radio Drama 1922–1928' published in *Sound Journal* and now available along with other articles via his website: www.savoyhill.co.uk/invisibleplay/index.html

There's also an account of the evolution of radio drama from early experiments in both the United States and Britain in the opening chapter of Tim Crook's *Radio Drama* published by Routledge.

Radio Drama: Scripts in Print

If you want to get hold of radio-drama scripts to read then the most available source is the BBC Writersroom website, which offers samples of interesting work which can be downloaded.

Hardly any radio scripts are currently in print, but there are a number of books which can be obtained fairly easily second hand or through libraries, which give some idea of the richness of the radio drama legacy.

Tom Stoppard's radio plays were collected in his *Plays: Two* published by Faber, available from online booksellers, while Anthony Minghella's *Cigarettes and Chocolate* can still be found in *Volume Two* of his *Collected Plays* published by

Methuen. Lee Hall's *Spoonface Steinberg* and *I Love You, Jimmy Spud* are in *Volume One* of his *Collected Plays* published by Methuen. *Not Talking* and *Contractions* (the stage version of *Love Contract*) are in Mike Bartlett's *Plays: One* published by Methuen. *Six Plays for Radio* by Giles Cooper, published by the BBC in 1966, is harder to find but offers examples of the work of one of the masters of radio drama.

It's still easy to find copies of the *Penguin New English Dramatists Volume 12: Radio Plays*, published in 1968, which includes plays by Caryl Churchill, Giles Cooper and C.P. Taylor. Also well worth seeking out are the volumes put out between 1978 and 1991 by Methuen of *Best Radio Plays of the Year: The Giles Cooper Award Winners*. Writers whose work can be found in the series include Harold Pinter, Tom Stoppard, Anthony Minghella, John Arden, Peter Tinniswood, David Pownall, Peter Barnes, William Trevor, Olwen Wymark and Fay Weldon.

Stephen Wyatt's *Memorials to the Missing, Gerontius* and *R.I.P. Maria Callas: Monologues for Stage and Radio* are available on www.amazon.co.uk or from Lulu Publications at www.lulu.com.

Miscellaneous

Audio Drama Wiki audiodrama.wikia.com

A useful database for audio drama with entries on playwrights, plays, producers and actors

Audiotheque www.audiotheque.co.uk

The Audiotheque offers a forum for posting independently made short experimental pieces such as one-minute dramas for mobile phones and extemporised pieces as well as interviews with distinguished radio writers such as Mike Walker.

www.suttonelms.org.uk/RADIO1.HTML

A site which offers helpful and detailed checklists of radio plays and writers over the years plus articles on radio drama.

www.nickhernbooks.co.uk

 facebook.com/nickhernbooks

twitter.com/nickhernbooks